Jörg Hartenauer

Introduction to
Business Intelligence

Jörg Hartenauer

Introduction to Business Intelligence

Concepts and Tools

VDM Verlag Dr. Müller

ISBN: 978-3-8364-1806-5

Preface of the editors

Many students are writing excellent bachelor and master theses. But only a few of them acquire a bigger audience and play a major role on the book market.

The aim of the book series "Applied Business Information Systems" of the VDM publisher is to boost outstanding final theses in Business Information Systems by publishing the thesis as a book.

Business Intelligence is not a new buzz word or gadget for IT-Managers. It is a necessary tool to collect, to sort and to analyse corporate data. Mr Hartenauer describes the elementary facts, structures, key words and coherences in his book. It's a compact and informative guide on Business Intelligence.

We recommend it to everybody who is looking for a well-founded introduction or refreshment in modern analytical methods.

The editors thank Mr Hartenauer for his engagement being sure that this book will offer a lot of readers a high benefit for their work or study.

Sankt Augustin (Germany), June 2007

Prof. Dr. Andreas Gadatsch   Prof. Dr. Dirk Schreiber

Table of Contents

List of Figures

List of Tables

List of Abbreviations

ACM	Association for Computer Machinery
B2B	Business-to-Business
B2C	Business-to-Consumer
B2E	Business-to-Employee
BI	Business Intelligence
BSC	Balanced Scorecard
CMS	Content Management System
Cp.	Compare
CRM	Customer Relationship Management
DB	Data-Base
DBMS	Data-Base Management System
DM	Data Mart
DMS	Document Management System
DW	Data Warehouse
EII	Enterprise Information Integration
EIP	Enterprise Information Portal
EIS	Executive Information System
ERP	Enterprise Resource Planning
Et seq./seqq.	And the following page/and the following pages
ETL	Extraction, Transformation, Loading
HTML	HyperText Markup Language
Ibid.	Ibidem = at the same place
IT	Information Technology
J2EE/Java EE	Java Platform, Enterprises Edition
KDD	Knowledge Discovery in Databases
KM	Knowledge Management
KPI	Key Performance Indicator
MDBMS	Multidimensional Data-Base Management System
MIS	Management Information System
MOLAP	Multidimensional On-Line Analytical Processing
MS	Microsoft
ODS	Operational Data Store
OLAP	On-Line Analytical Processing
OLE DB	Object Linking and Embedding Database

OLTP	On-Line Transactional Processing
p./pp.	page/pages
RDBMS	Relational Data-Base Management System
ROLAP	Relational On-Line Analytical Processing
SQL	Structured Query Language
WISU	Wirtschaftsstudium (German periodical)
XML	Extended Query Language

Glossary

Ad-hoc-Query / Reporting	Irregular and not standardised creation of queries and reports in order to solve business pro-lems/answer ad hoc questions by the means of different Business Intelligence tools such as *Data Mining* and *OLAP*
Back-end-tool	Part of a (business intelligence) system which does not directly interact with the user of this system, e.g., ETL-tools in the context of a Data Warehouse
Business Intelligence	(BI) The IT supported process with the stages of collecting, organising, storing, and distributing inter-nal and external data and information with the pur-pose of gaining competitive advantages
BI-system	The company-specific set of tools, processes and organisational issues co-operating in the process of business intelligence
BI-tool	Generic term for any method or purchased/self-developed application used on different stages of the BI-process; each tool-category comprises one or more application(s)
Cube	Multidimensional view on a set of data. Each axis of the multidimensional cube represents one dimen-sion and its instances; data values (measures or facts) are represented by the intersections of the different instances
Data Mart	A functional oriented database (often MDBMS) which is populated with data from the *data ware-house* and is optimised for the analytical purposes of one specific group of users
Data Mining	Undirected exploration of great amounts of data by the means of statistical and other methods with the purpose of generating new knowledge
Data Redundancy	Repeated storage of the same data in different tables of one (ore even several) database(s)
Data Warehouse	Broad collection of a company's internal and exter-nal data in one database with data history and in a companywide agreed and consistent structure

ETL	Extraction, Transformation and Loading of internal and external data from different (operational) sources into one single database, i.e., *Data Ware-house* or *ODS*
Front-end-tool	Part of a (business intelligence) system, that the user of this system directly interacts with, e.g., reporting or data mining tools
Information Retrieval	Representation, organisation, storage of, and access to information
Knowledge Management	(KM), a system of activities and applications which facilitate the utilisation of the knowledge of an organisation by its members
MDBMS	Multidimensional database management system; a database that physically stores data in the form of a multidimensional (hyper-)*cube*
Metadata	"Data about data", data that describes the structure, the content, keys and indexes of other data (data model)
OLE DB-DM	(Object Linking and Embedding Database for Data Mining), extension of the SQL query language; allows the user to train and test data mining models
RDBMS	Relational database management system; a database that stores data in manifold tables linked to each other by the means of key attributes. Data is stored in a normalised format in order to avoid *data redundancies*
Tuple	Specified element of a quantity or a single row of a table in a relational database

1   Motivation and Objectives of this Book

Fast changes in the economic environment and technological developments in the field of information technology (IT) constitute massive challenges for today's companies. Without the recognition and the management of these challenges business organisations might be threatened to be forced into a dominated competitive position.[1] Therefore the process of financial forecasting increasingly gains importance as only accurate forecasts enables a business to allocate its financial resources in an optimised manner.[2] The use of forecasting software might result in a better management of expenses, the improvement of factory order planning, and a simplification of project management and other capital spending.[3]

Business intelligence (BI) offers different concepts and tools to organisations and enables the business on the one hand to create the information needed for an accurate and reliable forecast and on the other hand even might disclose chances to improve existing processes. The exploration of currently being unknown relationships and associations between different variables in significant amounts of operational internal and external data, the creation of regular reports for different management levels and the possibility of processing individual queries for answering spontaneously occurring questions offer a wide range of chances for gaining new insides and knowledge. The tool set of BI enhances the business's ability to transform data into information and from there into knowledge.

This book introduces different theoretical concepts and definitions of business intelligence. Starting from there the most important IT tools which can be utilised in the process of generating new knowledge in an organisation are presented. As BI-tools are usually not used as single applications but rather in a complex system the relationships between these are evaluated as well.

---

[1] Cp.: Grothe, M./Gentsch, P. 2000, p. 22; Kemper, H.-G. et al. 2006, pp. 5 seqq.; Nölken, D. 2002, p. 2.
[2] Cp.: Perridon, L./Steiner, M. 2007, p. 651 et seq.
[3] Cp.: Whiting, R. 2002, p. 37.

2   Business Intelligence – Definitions and Concepts

The following part of the book evaluates the theoretical background of the broad range of topics linked to BI. Different definitions and concepts are introduced and examined and an architectural framework is outlined. A collection of the most valuable tools and their concepts used in the context of BI and information retrieval is presented as well.

2.1   Data, Information, Knowledge, and Intelligence

Business intelligence is meant for enabling companies to gain new knowledge from and explore before unknown patterns or relations in today's masses of internal and external data. Therefore a distinction between the terms *data, information, knowledge,* and *intelligence* should be made before the investigation of BI-concepts.

Raw **data** are symbols such as letters or figures or letters with syntax, i.e., symbols in a specified and meaningful order instead of an arbitrary one.[4] An example (based on Grothe/Gentsch)[5] for data are the figures of the increasing enumeration at the rotary switch of a cooktop (e.g., '1' to '6'). But data contains little value for a company as long as it does not undergo any kind of processing[6] or some kind of interpretation. The recognition of the relation between the position of the switch and the temperature is the process establishing the difference between pure data and **information**. Making the prediction that a glowing light at the switch means a hot surface or just being cautious because of the switch being activated on level "6" can be seen as pattern-based **knowledge**. The last step to **intelligence** would then be a thorough understanding of the physical processes which cause the heating of the cooktop. These differences and the evaluation from data to knowledge and to intelligence are illustrated in figure 1 below.

---

[4] Cp.: Gadatsch, A. 2005, p. 300, and Grothe, M./Gentsch, P. 2000, p. 18, and Keyes, J. 2006, p.13 seq.
[5] Cp.: Grothe, M./Gentsch, P. 2000, p. 18.
[6] Cp.: Devine, P. W. et al. 2004, pp. 21 – 39, here: p. 27.

Figure 1: From Information to Intelligence

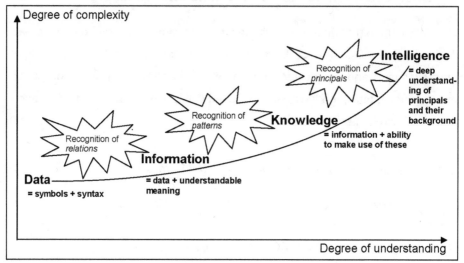

Source: Adapted from Grothe, M./Gentsch, P. 2000, p. 18 and Gadatsch, A. 2005, p. 300 (trans-lated by the author)

The recognition of relations, patterns and principals is not yet possible (only) by the means of information technologies. Especially the interpretation of principals (for instance as an outcome of data mining) compellingly requires human intelligence as management decisions are typically based on the exchange and conversations between humans and not (artificial) machines.[7]

2.2 Structure of Data

An additional distinction has to be made between structured and unstructured data. According to Devine et al. **structured data** are usually quantitative data with some form of inherent structure or logical arrangement[8] and are often available as a tabular format, i.e., organised in rows and columns, such as in spreadsheets or regular databases.[9] But only an estimated proportion of 15% of all business information exists in this structured manner.[10] That means that 85% of data (and therefore also the inherent information) are hidden in an **unstructured** form, i.e., data that appear to lack any order or categorisation such as

---

[7] Cp.: Maluf, D. et al. 2006, pp. 248 – 257, here: p. 248.
[8] Cp.: Devine, P. W. et al. 2004, pp. 21 – 39, here: p. 32.
[9] Cp.: Devine, P. W. et al. 2004, pp. 21 – 39, here: p. 27.
[10] Cp.: Blumberg, R./Atre, S., 12.03.2007, www.dmreview.com.

text documents, presentations, meetings, conversations, notes from call centres, web pages, and pictures.[11] Although such qualitative information are of significant importance especially for a company's strategic decisions the provision of business's executives with these data is often uncoordinated and inefficient;[12] this might also be caused by the fact that tools and techniques that successfully transform structured data into knowledge and intelligence are not yet capable of processing unstructured data in the same efficient way.[13]

Metadata (i.e., data about data)[14], for instance the author's name, the time of creation or tags describing the content, can be used to reveal information about an unstructured document.[15] As these metadata can be stored in a structured format such as a table in a relational database, the more correct term for this type of data might be **semi-structured data**.[16]

2.3 Definitions and Concepts of Business Intelligence

A single and consistent definition of the term "Business Intelligence" does not exist. Different authors focus on several different aspects and develop their own scope on this topic. In general two main approaches can be distinguished: On the one hand there exists a technologically dominated and application focussed view but on the other hand there is a more holistic approach centring on the process of generating and distributing BI in business organisations.[17]

Kemper ascribes the primary approach to the definition of "business intelligence" to a report of the Gartner Group published in 1996.[18] This report assumes that being leading in a competitive marketplace is the key to an enter-

---

[11] Cp. for more examples: Devine, P. W. et al. 2004, pp. 21 – 39, here: p. 33; Bange, C. 2004, p. 1; Blumberg, R./Atre, S., 12.03.2007, www.dmreview.com.
[12] Cp.: Bange, C. 2004, p. 1.
[13] Cp.: Blumberg, R./Atre, S., 12.03.2007, www.dmreview.com.
[14] Cp.: Devine, P. W. et al. 2004, pp. 21 – 39, here: p. 36.
[15] Please refer also to chapter 3.8 "Metadata Management" for the role of metadata in the context of BI and DW.
[16] Cp.: Blumberg, R./Atre, S., 12.03.2007, www.dmreview.com.; similar: Devine, P. W. et al. 2004, pp. 21 – 39, here: p. 34.
[17] Cp.: Oehler, K. 2006, p. 2.
[18] Cp.: Kemper, H.-G. et al. 2006, p. 2.

prise's further growth and wealth.[19] The basis for sound business decisions should rather be accurate and current information on the enterprise's situation than pure intuition.[20] At that point, BI is mainly seen as a set of different applications supporting information retrieval in business organisations: "Data analysis, reporting, and query tools can help business users to wade through a sea of data to synthesize valuable information from it – today these tools collectively fall into a category called 'business intelligence'."[21]

BI is seen by Bange as a synonym for "**tools** for the collection, storage, formatting and presentation of internal quantitative data that reflects the company's experiences and its relevant environment".[22] In a similar technologically focused way BI is introduced by a range of different other authors.[23]

In contrast, a holistic approach is taken by Grothe and Gentsch: They describe BI as an **analytic process** which transforms fragmented internal and external competitive data into action targeted knowledge about the abilities, positions, actions and objectives of the observed internal or external fields of activities (actors and processes).[24]

Knobloch offers a similar view, even though he distinguishes between the process of data acquisition, data preparation, data analysis, and data presentation on the one hand and the BI techniques, tools and concepts which are used in this process on the other hand.[25]

Kemper himself defines BI as an integrated, organisation specific, IT-based approach to managerial decision support.[26] Although he offers a holistic and company specific perspective, there is also a strange addition to his point of

---

[19] Cp.: Gartner Group 1996 in Anandarajan, A. et al. 2004, p. 19.
[20] Cp.: ibid.
[21] Ibid.
[22] Bange, C. 2004, p. 69 (translated by the author).
[23] Cp. for example: Nölken, D. 2002, p. 233; Hannig, U. 2002, p. 6; Keyes, J. 2006, p. 155., Anandarajan, A. et al. 2004, pp. 1 – 20, here: p. 19.
[24] Cp.: Grothe, M./Gentsch, P. 2000, p. 19.
[25] Cp.: Knobloch, C. 2005, p. 18 seq.
[26] Cp.: Kemper, H.-G. et al. 2006, p. 8.

view: as a "borderline to many other definitions"[27] he distinguishes between BI-*tools* which are exclusively used for the design of BI-*applications*. That means that in his opinion purchasable tools only assist in the development of company specific BI-applications of which each is only an aspect of the whole approach.[28]

Moss' and Atre's definition of BI being an "architecture and a collection of integrated operational as well as decision-support applications"[29] should be classified somewhere in the middle between the technology focussed approaches on the one side and the process orientated ones on the other side. Their definition implies a further perspective by the use of the terms "architecture" and "integrated" and does not only focus on a technical collection of applications.

Vitt et al. do not really offer a clear definition of BI but describe it as the "key to bringing together information, people and technology to successfully manage a company or organisation".[30] Although this is more a description than a definition of BI it shows an integrated and in a way process orientated view aiming at data as well as the users and the underlying technology.

2.4 Working Definition

Due to the fact that no consistent definition of BI exists and each definition focuses on specific aspects, a working definition will be developed by the author for the purpose of this book.

In this piece of work **business intelligence** is defined as the IT supported **process** with the stages of collecting, organising, storing, and distributing internal and external data and information[31] with the objective of:

---

[27] Ibid. (translated by the author).
[28] Cp.: ibid.
[29] Moss, L. T./Atre, S. 2003, p. 4.
[30] Vitt, E. et al. 2002, p. 13.
[31] "Internal" data is obtained from a company's own operational applications such as Enterprise Resource Planning (ERP)-systems or Customer Relationship Management (CRM)-applications whereas "external" data are gathered from sources that are in the company's environment and are not directly controlled by it [annotation of the author].

- getting new knowledge about the business,
- improving both the speed as well as the quality of decision-making, and
- gaining competitive advantages by the means of BI.

Within this process a variable set of different categorised **BI-tools** can be used on different stages of the BI-process as mentioned above. These tool catego- ries comprise various applications, for instance for the extraction, transformation and loading (ETL) of data from different operational sources into a data DW or for the process of data warehousing within the context of organising and storing data.

An **application** in the context of BI is any purchased or self-developed com- puter-program which belong to one of the tool categories.[32] Each application may be classified to and be used in one ore more of the tool categories.

A **BI-system** in this book labels the company-specific set of tools, (sub-) proc- esses and organisational issues co-operating in the process of BI.

Figure 2: Concept of the Working Definition

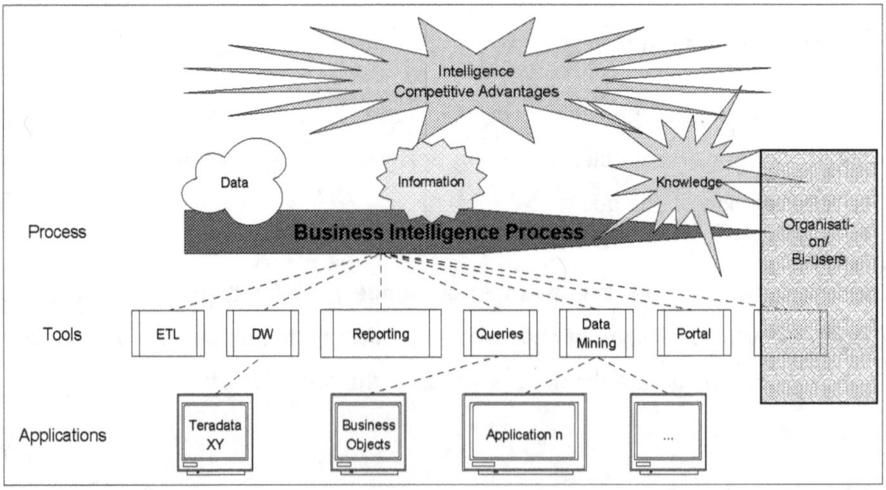

Source: Own illustration

---

[32] For instance, a data warehouse is a **tool** (category) for organising and storing data; the Teradata database is an **application** within the context of DW tools.

So, making use of BI in an enterprise always has to cover two aspects: on the one hand technological issues, i.e., for instance choosing the right tools and applications, and on the other hand a process perspective, i.e., the set-up and implementation of efficient business processes that optimise the usefulness of the tools.

2.5 Business Intelligence Architectural Frameworks

There are not only various definitions of BI in scientific literature but there are also attempts to set up an assortative or architectural framework for business intelligence tools. In order to structure the introduction of BI-tools in the following chapter, three of these frameworks are presented and their main differences are critically evaluated. The first is a technologically focused approach, the second one is process-orientated and the last framework is a layer model.

2.5.1 Technological Approach

Dittmar and Gluchowski take a technologically focused approach in order to categorise the various BI-tools.[33] They distinguish between a narrow, an analysis-orientated, and a broad understanding of BI. The **narrow understanding** only incorporates Online Analytical Processing (OLAP) and Management Information Systems (MIS) respectively Executive Information Systems (EIS)[34] into the context of business intelligence. These tools are very firmly linked to the data management components of the BI system and mainly enable the preparation and presentation of multidimensionally organised data.[35] However, other front-end-tools such as those for ad-hoc-reporting or for data mining are explicitly excluded from this constricted understanding and belong according to Ditt-

---

[33] Cp.: Dittmar, C./Gluchowski, P. 2002, p. 32 et seqq.
[34] There is not a very sharp distinction between the terms management information system and executive information system: MISs are defined as reporting-orientated analysis-systems focused on planning and controlling the operational value-adding processes and mostly used by the lower and middle management; EISs on the other hand are consequently targeted at the company's top-management and their requirements of information (Cp.: Kemper, H.-G. et al. 2006, p. 114 et seq.). However, as the data source for both is ideally a common one, such as a data warehouse, the difference is only on the presentation layer. For the purposes of this book is therefore no distinction made between MIS and EIS [annotation of the author].
[35] Cp.: Dittmar, C./Gluchowski, P. 2002, p. 33.

mar/Gluchowski to the slightly wider **analysis-orientated perspective.**[36] Other tools that they include into this understanding are analytical Customer Relationship Management (CRM) systems, planning and consolidation tools and applications for the measurement of key performance indicators (KPI) or the implementation of a Balanced Scorecard (BSC). In this classification other important tools such as ETL-components, data warehouses and standardised reporting fall only in their even wider **broad understanding of BI.**[37]

Even though this framework is a first step in order to help classifying and organising tools and methods in the context of BI, some fundamental weaknesses inhere in it. The distinction between MIS/EIS and other tools as described above is not very sharp especially considering the fact that the scope of MIS/EIS is not specified in more depth. In addition, it does not imply at all which and how to use the tools mentioned and how they are linked to each other. Figure 3 below illustrates this classification.

Figure 3: Classification of BI-tools according to Dittmar/Gluchowski

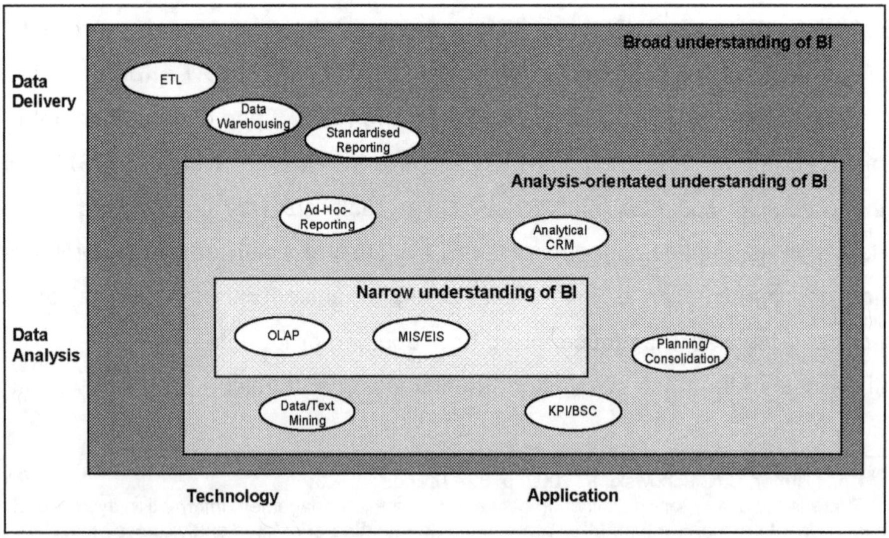

Source: Dittmar, C./Gluchowski, P. 2002, p. 33 (translated and slightly adapted by the author)

---

[36] Cp.: ibid.
[37] Cp.: ibid.

2.5.2 Process-Orientated Approach

Another approach is described by Grothe and Gentsch:[38] As stated in chapter 2.3, the analytic process is in the scope of their definition of business intelligence. Based upon this their structure of the manifold tools is a process-orientated one. They phase BI into three consecutive stages:[39]

1) Data delivery/data provision
2) Discovery of relations, patterns, and principles
3) Knowledge sharing/communication

Starting from these process stages, the classification of methods and tools results in table 1 below.[40]

Table 1: Classification of BI-tools and BI-methods according to Grothe/Gentsch

	Internal, market relevant and competitive data	
Characteristics of fundamental data:	*Generally quantitative ...*	*... quantitative and qualitative*
	Structured ...	*... barely structured*
Process of discovery:	*Based on hypotheses ...*	*... generally no hypotheses*
1) Data delivery	• Operational systems (Online transactional processing – OLTP)) • Data Warehouse/Data Mart • Multidimensional models (planning, budgeting, analysis, reporting)	• Internet/Intranet • Discussion forums • Implicit knowledge (human resources)
2) Discovery	• Multidimensional analyses (OLAP/SQL/MIS) • Balanced Scorecard • "Classical" methods (KPI, variance analysis, ABC-analysis, correlation analysis, etc.) • Business simulation	• Data mining • Text mining • Web mining • Case Based-Reasoning • Issue Management/early warning systematic
3) Knowledge sharing	• Organisational and (corporate) cultural promotion of knowledge sharing and knowledge transfer • Date **and** event triggered reporting (KMS/internet channel/pull and push of information/profiles of interests)	

Source: Grothe, M./Gentsch, P. 2000, p. 21 (translated and slightly adapted by the author).

---

[38] Cp.: Grothe, M./Gentsch, P. 2000, p. 19.
[39] Cp.: Grothe, M./Gentsch, P. 2000, p. 20 seq.
[40] Although not all of the methods and tools in this table will be described in this book, they should at least be mentioned in the context of this framework; details regarding all tools can be found in the cited literature [annotation of the author].

This depiction gives a more holistic picture and enables the reader to better link specific tools and methods to the different stages of the BI process or to common business situations. Also the distinction between structured and unstructured data on each process phase supports a differentiated orientation.[41]

2.5.3 Layer Approach

The last framework to be introduced is an architectural approach by Kemper et al.[42] Even though they emphasise the fact that the concrete design of a BI-system always has to be company-specific, they present a general framework consisting of the following three layers:[43]

1) Data provision
2) Generation/storage/distribution of information
3) Access to information

Figure 4: Architectural BI-framework by Kemper et al.

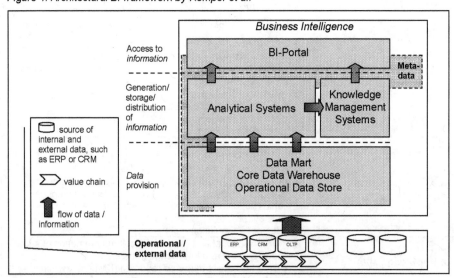

Source: own presentation based on and adapted from: Kemper, H.-G. et al 2006, p. 10 (translated by the author)

---

[41] Please refer to chapter 2.1 "Data, Information, Knowledge, and Intelligence" for the distinction of structured and unstructured respectively semi-structured data [annotation of the author].
[42] Cp.: Kemper, H.-G. et al. 2006, p. 10.
[43] Cp.: ibid.

In contrast to the process-oriented approach this framework does not include the provision of operational internal and external data into the context of BI. The operational OLTP-applications and external sources deliver raw data into the business intelligence system, but they would also exist without any BI-tools. The basis for successful BI-systems is consistent and high-quality data collected in DWs or operational data stores (ODSs) and further processed into data marts (DM).[44] The middle layer of the framework comprises tools for the generation of information and has also interfaces to knowledge management (KM) systems which are of significant importance for the storage and distribution of information, i.e., for instance, the outcomes of BI analyses.[45] A portal (especially focused on business intelligence) as a central point of access[46] supports the user-friendliness of a BI system and enhances the quantity and most likely the quality of the information generated.[47]

On the one hand Kemper presents an integrated view of a BI-system and also shows on the other hand (on a high level) the flow and transformation of data to information within this system. What has to be criticised in his approach is the fact that he gives examples on the data provision layer, but he is not as detailed on the middle layer and the access stage.[48]

From chapter 3 to chapter 7 this layer approach builds the framework to organise the introduction and description of the various BI-tools.

2.6 Real-Time Business Intelligence

A more recent development in the context of BI is striving for a real-time enterprise by the support of BI-tools. As the competition becomes stronger and stronger speed is the crucial factor of success.[49] Faster access to information

---

[44] Cp.: Kemper, H.-G. et al. 2006, p. 10 et seq.
[45] Cp.: Kemper, H.-G. et al. 2006, p. 11.
[46] Cp.: ibid.
[47] The term "portal" and its importance within the context of BI will be evaluated in more depth in chapter 7.3 "Business Intelligence Portal" [annotation of the author].
[48] Cp.: figure 4 on the previous page .
[49] Cp.: Auer, U. 2004, pp. 34 – 35, here: p. 34.

("at a thought's speed"[50]) might be the basis for competitive differentiators.[51] However, depending on the business situation which is in focus of the specific business intelligence (sub-)process, "real-time" does not necessarily has to be taken literally, but "right-time" appears to be the more appropriate term.[52] While some situations require close to real-time actions, a delay of timely information of several minutes or even hours might be acceptable in other cases.[53]

The aim of right-time BI is always to minimise the period between an incidence with impact on the business and the appropriate reaction, i.e., making adequate decisions and taking the right actions.[54] This latency consists of three phases: **data latency** is the time between any event and its recording in a DW, **analysis latency** means the period of data analysis and distribution of information to the appropriate decision-maker; the time required for the understanding of the information and making the decision respectively initialising any action is called **decision latency**.[55] The longer it takes until an action is conducted the less is its value, therefore right-time BI addresses as well the recording of events as their easily understandable presentation and thereby indirectly the time of making the decision. White identifies four areas that have to be considered in this context:[56]

- right-time data integration,
- right-time data reporting,
- right-time performance management, and
- right-time automated actions.

These four categories address the phases of latency as described above: right-time data integration reduces data latency, reporting and the measurement and

---

[50] Vitt, E. et al. 2002, p. 15 et seqq.
[51] Cp.: ibid.
[52] Cp.: White, C. 22.01.2007, www.dmreview.com.
[53] Cp.: ibid.
[54] Cp.: Auer, U. 2004, pp. 34 – 35, here: p. 35; Oehler, K. 2006, p. 48.
[55] Cp.: ibid.
[56] Cp.: White, C. 22.01.2007, www.dmreview.com.

management of the performance of a company support the minimisation of analyses gaps while automated actions address decision latency.

Another approach to reduce data latency is the direct access of analytical tools to data in operational databases (and DWs) in the context of enterprise informa- tion integration (EII)[57]; so called low- (or zero-) latency (operational) data is accessed via an EII-server instead of or complementary to a classical DW.[58] This EEI approach shows significant parallelisms to the concept of a virtual data warehouse.[59] However, a direct access to the operational databases most likely causes performance problems within the OLTP-applications and inconsisten- cies between different data structures;[60] therefore this approach is not favoured by the majority of authors.[61]

There exist manifold tools for supporting and conducting the process of BI. Starting with the data provision layer of Kemper's BI-framework[62] the following chapters evaluate the most important of those. The tools are introduced and their meaning for BI and their classification in the layers of the framework are discussed.

---

[57] Cp.: Klaus, A. 2006, pp. 26 – 27, here: p. 27; White, C. 22.01.2007, www.dmreview.com.
[58] Cp.: White, C. 22.01.2007, www.dmreview.com and also chapter 3 "Data Warehouse".
[59] Cp.: Gadatsch, A. 2005, p. 297; Bange, C. 2004, p. 71. Please refer also to chapter 3.5 "Central Data Warehouse and Data Marts" for possible architectural approaches of a DW [anno- tation of the author].
[60] Cp. for examples of inconsistencies based on different data structures chapter 3.7 "Extrac- tion, Transformation, Loading – Data Upload and Cleansing" of this book.
[61] Cp. for example: Grothe, M./Gentsch, P. 2000, p. 53; Inmon, W. H. 2005, p. 11 et seqq.; Dittmar, C./Gluchowski, P. 2002, p. 35; Gadatsch, A. 2005, p. 297; Nölken, D. 2002, p. 251; Kemper, H.-G./Lee, P. 2002, p. 17.
[62] Cp.: Kemper, H.-G. et al. 2006, p. 10 and also chapter 2.5.3 "Layer Approach" of this book.

3   Data Warehouse

As it becomes of more and more importance to systematically utilise the knowl-edge that is stored in the company's data in order to gain or to secure market shares,[63] a single consistent and (from operational systems) independent data-base as a data provision component[64] for analytical applications is aspired. Objective is to find the important pieces of information in a flood of data lacking the information that really is decision-relevant.[65] This database is the data warehouse. The basic idea of a DW is the separation of transactional orientated operational data (outside the DW) and those used for analytical processes and management information systems.[66] The parallelisms between a physical ware-house (store) and a data warehouse are summarised in table 2:

Table 2: Analogy between Physical Warehouse and Data Warehouse

	Physical Warehouse	**Data Warehouse**
Function	Physical storing of goods	Digital storing of data
Content	Goods stored by type, quality and volumes	Data stored by type, structure and volume
Objective of warehouse's organisation	Short time of stock removal for the recipient of the good	Short time of access to data for the user
Topicality	Regular supply of goods	Regular update of data

Source: Gadatsch, A. 2005, p. 296 (translated and slightly adapted by the author).

3.1   Definition

The classical definition of the term 'data warehouse' is made by Inmon: "A data warehouse is a **subject-oriented**, **integrated**, **non-volatile**, and **time-variant** collection of data in support of managements decisions."[67] The DW comprises granular corporate data, i.e., very detailed and easily accessible data, so that it can be used for manifold purposes within a company.[68]

---

[63] Cp.: Gehra et al. 2005, pp. 236 – 242, here p. 236.
[64] Please also refer to chapter 2.5.3 "Layer Approach".
[65] Cp.: Grothe, M./Gentsch, P. 2000, p. 51.
[66] Cp.: Dippold et al. 2005, p. 188.
[67] Inmon, W. H. 2005, p. 29, accentuations by the author of the book. Although this is a recent publication, Inmon used the same definition already in the editions before the fourth one, cp. for instance: Knobloch, C. 2005, p. 340, who refers the same definition to Inmon's first edition of this book (published in 1996) [annotation of the author].
[68] Cp.: Inmon, W. H. 2005, p. 29.

3.2   Characteristics

The **subject-orientation** distinguishes the DW from functional OLTP-applications. These are optimised for specific functional areas whereas typical subjects of a DW comprise customer, product, vendor, bill of material, etc. Each branch and each company does have a specific set of typical subjects.[69]

The feature of **integration** manifests in the consolidation of data from different operational sources.[70] Inmon sees in this characteristic the most important one of a DW.[71] During the process of loading data from multiple and disparate sources into the DW, data are converted, summarised, re-sequenced, etc. in order to provide a single physical corporate image.[72] This process of extraction, transformation and loading (ETL) will be subject of chapter 3.7.

Data which are stored in a DW are – in contrast to data in operational systems, i.e., OLTP-applications – **non-volatile**. A DW's data are not further processed or changed but only accessed for analytical purposes.[73] That does not necessarily mean, that a customer's credit ranking for example is uploaded once and never changed. There are in fact as many credit ranking entries linked to this customer as this customer has had during his business connexions with this company, but each one has a time-specific validity, i.e., a "valid from" and a "valid to" date.[74] In contrast, data which are still processed in OLTP-applications are designated and optimised for regular updates and changes. In an operational system, for instance, only the current status of a customer's credit ranking can usually be found.

The fourth important characteristic is the **time-variancy** of a DW. Every piece of data is accurate for some moment in time, it is always some kind of snapshot in a 'static' format.[75] Data is not updated in a classical sense of understanding, but

---

[69] Cp.: ibid.
[70] Cp.: Humm; B./Wietek, F. 2005, pp. 3 -14, here: p. 3.
[71] Cp.: Inmon W. H. 2005, p. 30.
[72] Cp.: ibid.
[73] Cp.: Humm, B./Wietek, F. 2005, pp. 3 -14, here: p. 3.
[74] Cp.: Inmon, W. H. 2005, p. 105 et seq.
[75] Cp.: Inmon, W. H. 2005, p. 32.

a new snapshot as described above is written. The time horizon of a DW is therefore longer (5 – 10 years) than of an OLTP-application (current to 60 – 90 days), and the key structure of a DW always reflects that element of time.[76]

3.3 Key Terms

Before analysing the structure of data in a DW some important terms are to be introduced. Independent of using a relational or a multidimensional database,[77] the data always have to be described as a basis for all analytical processes.[78] There have to be distinguished between three important aspects: Measures, dimensions, and hierarchy of dimensions.

Measures – also synonymously called **facts** – are the smallest piece of information in a DW.[79] They represent numerical values which can be aggregated or be used for the calculation of other more complex measures.[80] Kemper emphasis that facts are – from a semantical point of view – managerial KPIs.[81]

Dimensions in this context are of a more descriptive nature.[82] They form a multidimensional co-ordinate system for the user's navigation within the data and therefore can be used as a filter or as analytical criteria for measures. One dimension consists of several instances which are hierarchally arranged.[83] Typical instances of the dimension 'time' are for example days, months and years. Dimensions can be aggregated along their instances, for example days to weeks, weeks to months, etc. This structure is the so-called **'hierarchy of dimensions'**.[84]

---

[76] Cp.: Ibid.; also Humm, B./Wietek, F. 2005, pp. 3 -14, here: p. 4.
[77] Please refer to the following chapter 3.4 "Relational and Multidimensional Model" for the details of these data structures.
[78] Cp.: Humm, B./Wietek, F. 2005, pp. 3 -14, here: p. 5.
[79] Cp.: ibid.; Kemper, H.-G. et al. 2006, p. 61.
[80] Cp.: ibid.; Humm , B./Wietek, F. (2005, pp. 3 – 14, here p. 5) distinguish between "measures" (e.g., revenue in US-$)and "instance of a measure" (e.g., 100,000). However, as they also point out the synonymous use of "measure" and "fact" and other authors do not make use of this extremely accurate distinction, it will not be further used in this book [annotation of the author].
[81] Cp.: Kemper, H.-G. et al. 2006, p. 61.
[82] Cp.: Kemper, H.-G. et al. 2006, p. 62.
[83] Cp.: Humm, B./Wietek, F. 2005, pp. 3 -14, here: p. 5.
[84] Ibid. and Bange, C. 2004, p. 91.

A **cube** (sometimes also called 'hyper-cube') is a multidimensional array defined by three to n dimensions.[85] Each fact (measure) is specified by one instance on each dimensional axis; measures are the points of intersections of the axes.[86] Figure 5 below illustrates the relationships of cube, dimensions, and measures.

Figure 5: Cube, Dimensions, and Measures

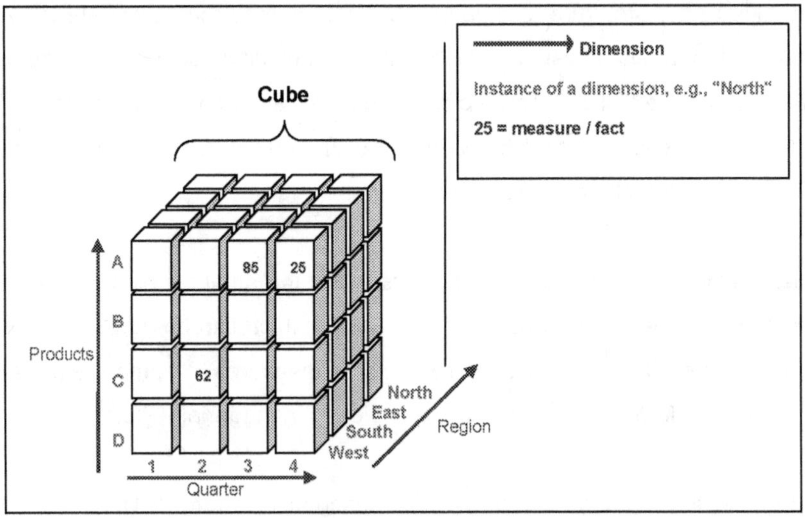

Source: Adapted from Bange, C. 2004, p. 91

3.4 Relational and Multidimensional Model

Although there are generally two different approaches discussed in literature how to store and organise data in a data warehouse – on the one hand the relational model and on the other hand the multidimensional approach[87] – the definitions of and the distinctions between these two concepts are inconsistent. Therefore this chapter not only introduces the two models but also points out the literature's main overlaps and contradictions.

The **relational model** is the basic approach for the architecture of a DW and reflects the classical database design as developed and introduced by Codd at

---

[85] Cp.: Bange, C. 2004 p. 79 and Weber, J. et al. .1999, p. 22.
[86] Cp.: Weber, J. et al. 1999, p. 22.
[87] Cp.: Inmon, W. H. 2005, p. 357; Keyes, J. 2006 p. 101 et seq.; Bange, C. 2004 p. 75; Kemper, A./Eickler, A. 2006 p. 511.

the beginning of the 1970s.[88] In this database-model data are stored in tables and organised in columns and rows.[89] The tables are linked with each other by keys, such as unique customer numbers or store identifiers.[90] Data in relational databases ideally exist in a normalised form, i.e., on a very granular level of detail and without any redundancies.[91] The most important advantages of a relational database management system (RDBMS) as introduced above are:[92]

- Versatility of analysis (very granular, detailed data),
- Stability for high volumes of data,
- Clarity of meaning, and
- High scalability.

Inseparably connected to the relational approach is the technique of accessing the data stored in a database organised in this manner: the structured query language (SQL) usually is the tool to interface from applications to the data.[93]

The **multidimensional model** for database design is described in different ways. On the one hand there are authors who postulate that the multidimensional cube as described in chapter 3.3 is directly reflected in the storage structure of the database[94] and on the other hand Inmon's approach which will be discussed later in this chapter.[95]

The multidimensional storage indicates that the whole data cube with its aggregated sums and probably derived KPIs is physically implemented in the DW. Advantages of such a multidimensional database management system

---

[88] Cp. Codd, E. 1970, pp. 377 – 387, cited from Bange, C. 2004, p. 81. For a very detailed introduction of the relational model refer to: Kemper, A./Eickler, A. 2006 p. 261 et seqq.
[89] Cp. for example: Inmon, W. H. 2005, p. 357 et seqq. and Dippold, R. et al. 2005, p. 204 and Kemper, A./Eickler, A. 2006, p. 69 et seqq.
[90] Cp.: Inmon, W. H. 2005, p. 358.
[91] Cp.: Kemper, H.-G. et al. 2006, p. 58; regarding the process of normalisation: Kemper, A./Eickler, A. 2006, p. 181 et seqq. **"Data Redundancy"** is the repeated storage of the same data in different tables of a database, cp.: Kemper, A./Eickler, A. 2006, p. 17.
[92] Cp.: Inmon, W. H. 2005, p. 359; Humm, B./Wietek, F. 2005, pp. 3 -14, here: p. 8. and Nölken, D. 2002 p. 249.
[93] Cp.: ibid. and in more detail: Kemper, A./Eickler, A. 2006, p. 107 et seqq.
[94] Cp. for instance: Humm, B./Wietek, F. 2005, pp. 3 -14, here: p. 8; Bange, C. 2004, p. 93; Nölken, D. 2002, p. 248 et seqq.; Dippold, R. et al. 2005, p. 204 et seq.
[95] Please refer to page 23 of this book for Inmon's approach [annotation of the author].

(MDBMS) are a higher performance due to the pre-aggregation of data and a more intuitive navigation for the end-user who are not obliged to process (relatively) complex queries via SQL.[96] However, disadvantages (in comparison to a RDBMS) are the smaller storage capability of such a database[97] and problems caused by the fact that not every combination of the dimensional instances carries a value.[98]

One significant difference between the relational and the multidimensional model has to be emphasised at this point: data stored in a RDBMS are not optimised for any given purpose or set of processing requirements[99] and are therefore a flexible basis for manifold different analytical processes. The higher performance for a given set of requirements, in contrast, that can be achieved by the use of a MDBMS, has to be measured against the later inflexibility of this approach.

One approach to model the data of a DW is the so called star scheme and the associated snowflake scheme. The majority of authors align this approach to a physical storage of data in a relational DBMS;[100] Inmon, however, refers to the star scheme as a *multidimensional database* approach.[101] After introducing the star scheme and the snowflake scheme, the definition which best fits this book's purpose will be discussed.[102]

3.4.1 The Star Scheme

The so called **star scheme** is a typical data model for a DW architecture and is characterised by one fact table (such as "sales transactions") and surrounding dimension tables of which each one reflects an attribute of the fact table. As

---

[96] Cp.: Humm, B./Wietek, F. 2005, pp. 3 -14, here: p. 8; Nölken, D. 2002, p. 247; Bange, C. 2004, p. 79.
[97] Cp.: Humm, B./Wietek, F. 2005, pp. 3 -14, here: p. 8.
[98] This problem is also referred to as "hypersparsity", cp.: Nölken, D. 2002, p. 248.
[99] Cp.: Inmon, W. H. 2005, p. 127.
[100] Cp. for example: Dippold, R. et al. 2005, p. 205; Kemper, A./Eickler, A. 2006, p. 496 et seqq.; Humm, B./Wietek, F. 2005, pp. 3 -14, here: p. 8.
[101] Cp.: Inmon, W. H. 2005, p. 360.
[102] Please refer to page 23 of this book [annotation of the author].

figure 6 below illustrates, the arrangement of the dimension tables around the fact table might remind of a star which explains the name of this scheme.[103]

Figure 6: The Star Scheme

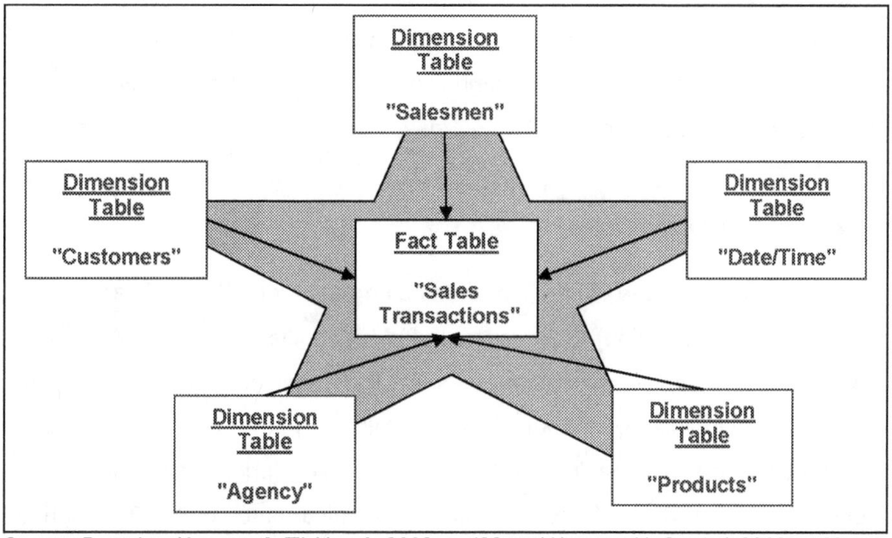

Source: Based on Kemper, A./Eickler, A. 2006, p. 498 and Kemper, H.-G. et al. 2006, p. 63

The amount of data occurrences (or tuples) in a fact table – such as specified sales in this example – is significant higher than data occurrences in a dimension table.[104] The fact table (compare table 3 below) contains columns which reflect the surrounding dimensions as information carrying attributes:[105]

Table 3: Example of the Fact Table "Sales Transactions"

Sales Transactions					
Date	**Agency**	**Product**	**Quantity**	**Customer**	**Salesman**
12.11.2006	Germany	4711	1	911	258
13.11.2006	Belgium	0815	25	852	468
...	...	...	...	...	...

Source: Based on Kemper, A./Eickler, A. 2006, p. 499 (translated and adapted by the author)

Each dimension table itself contains tuples explaining the entries in the fact tables (such as the customer number as an identifier). Therefore the star

---

[103] Cp.: Kemper, H.-G. et al. 2006, p. 63.
[104] Cp.: Inmon, W. H. 2005, p. 360 et seq. and Kemper, A./Eickler, A. 2006, p. 497.
[105] Cp.: Kemper, H.-G. et al. 2006, p. 63. The example introduced in this book is based on Kemper, A./Eickler, A. 2006, p. 499.

scheme is nothing else than a subject-oriented data model of a relational database. However, in contrast to the postulation of normalised and atomic data in a relational database (ideally in the 3rd normal form),[106] the star scheme deliberately utilises controlled redundancies (especially functional references within each table) in the dimension tables.[107] This controlled infringement of the 3rd normal form is accepted due to a higher performance and a reduction of complexity in the process of conducting queries.[108]

3.4.2 The Snowflake Scheme

The normalisation of the dimension tables along the hierarchies of each dimension results in (dimension) tables surrounded by additional ones.[109] When each of the dimension tables is encircled by several normalised tables, this structure reminds of a snowflake, as figure 7 on the following page illustrates. Although data redundancies are avoided and the size of each (prior not normalised) dimension table is reduced,[110] performance and maintenance of the DW might be suffering due to more tables that have to be joined in queries and have to be administrated in the processes of maintenance.[111]

---

[106] Cp.: Kemper, A./Eickler, A. 2006, p. 181 et seqq.
[107] Cp.: Kemper, H.-G. et al. 2006, p. 63.
[108] Cp.: ibid.; Kemper, A./Eickler, A. 2006, p. 498; Humm, B./Wietek, F. 2005, pp. 3 -14, here: p. 8.
[109] Cp.: Humm, B./Wietek, F. 2005, pp. 3 -14, here: p. 8.
[110] Cp.: Moss, L. T./Atre, S. 2003, p. 200.
[111] Cp.: ibid.; Humm, B./Wietek, F. 2005, pp. 3 -14, here: p. 8.; Kemper, H.-G. et al. 2006, p. 64 et seq.

Figure 7: The Snowflake Scheme

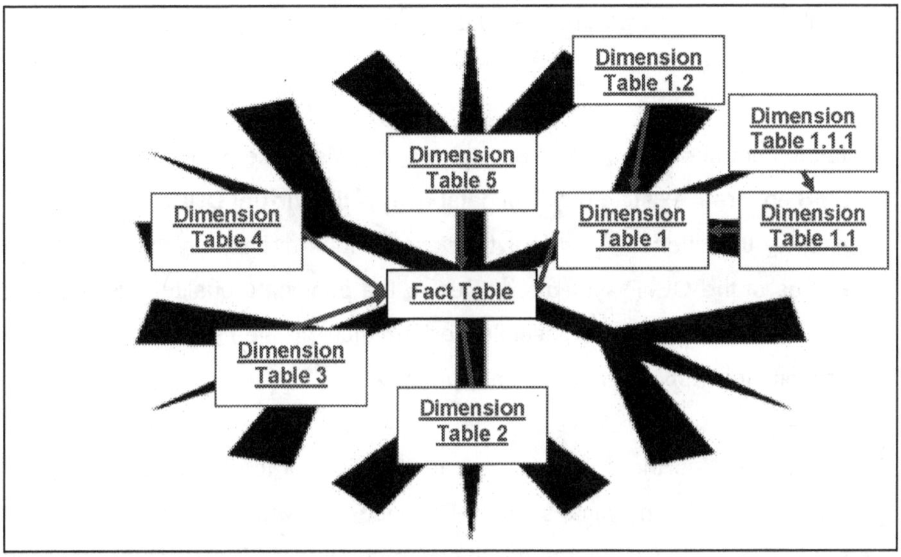

Source: Own presentation based on Moss, L. T./Atre, S. 2003, p. 200

Inmon does not only define the star scheme contradicting to the majority of authors (as indicated before) but also interprets the snowflake scheme in a slightly different way: In his opinion a snowflake structure is not the normalisation of dimension tables, but it accrues when more than one fact table is combined in a database[112] using the same dimension tables.[113]

For the purpose of this book (and according to the majority of authors) the star scheme and the snowflake scheme are referred to be a modelling approach to reflect multidimensional structures in a RDBMS; a MDBMS in contrast physically reflects the structure of a data cube in a multidimensional array.

3.5 Central Data Warehouse and Data Marts

There are basically three approaches to the system architecture of a DW in a business environment:[114]

---

[112] Cp.: Inmon, W. H. 2005, p. 361 et seq.
[113] A structure like the one described is also referred to as a "galaxy", joining several "stars" using the same dimension tables, compare for example: Kemper, H.-G. et al. 2006, p. 64 [annotation of the author].
[114] Cp.: Bange, C. 2004, p. 71; Gadatsch, A. 2005, p. 297 et seqq.

- the virtual data warehouse,
- the central data warehouse, and
- data marts.

While the central data warehouse – as well as DMs – use either a RDBMS or a MDBMS on a real existing physical database,[115] the **virtual DW** is a middleware channelling the queries[116] of analytical applications directly on the operational databases of the OLTP-systems.[117] Due to the poor data quality (missing data history, redundancies) and possible performance problems within the OLTP-applications this approach is not really practicable.[118]

The **central DW** is the only storage area for all data loaded from operational databases into this analytical system. Because the amount of data stored in a central DW is usually very large (up to several terabytes[119]), it is usually realised as a RDBMS.[120] As outlined before, this approach is very flexible and therefore enables the DW to serve unknown needs as well as unknown users as it is not optimised for one specific purpose of analysis and contains data on a very granular level.[121] However, especially regarding large queries, this independent and flexible structure of a RDBMS deteriorates its performance.[122]

Data marts are databases which are usually functional oriented, i.e., they are dedicated for the service of one specific group of people such as the marketing department of a company.[123] Due to the fact that the users and their require-ments are known (or can at least be described) and stable, the amount of data stored in a DM is usually significantly smaller than in a core DW. The typical architecture for a DM is a MDBMS, as high performance on a smaller set of

---

[115] Cp. for example: Bange, C. 2004, p. 75 or Kemper, A./Eickler, A. 2006, p. 510 et seq.
[116] The analytical applications such as OLAP will be introduced in chapter 4 [annotation of the author].
[117] Cp.: Gadatsch, A. 2005, p. 297. This approach is related to the concept of EII, but this con-cept includes DWs and does not replace those, cp.: White, C. 22.01.2007, www.dmreview.com [annotation of the author].
[118] Cp.: ibid.
[119] Cp. for example: Nölken, D. 2002, p.260.
[120] Cp.: Kemper, A./Eickler, A. 2006, p. 510 et seq.; Inmon, W. H. 2005, p. 369.
[121] Cp.: Inmon, W. H. 2005, p. 366 et seqq.
[122] Cp.: Inmon, W. H. 2005, p. 127.
[123] Cp.: Inmon, W. H. 2005, p. 370.

data is in the focus.[124] For this better performance regarding response time, calculated sums and aggregated values are often stored within a DM and the atomic data used for this calculation might be ignored and not stored; therefore the granularity of data that can be found in a data mart is usually not as detailed as in a DW.[125]

Figure 8: Core Data Warehouse, Data Marts, and Virtual Data Warehouse

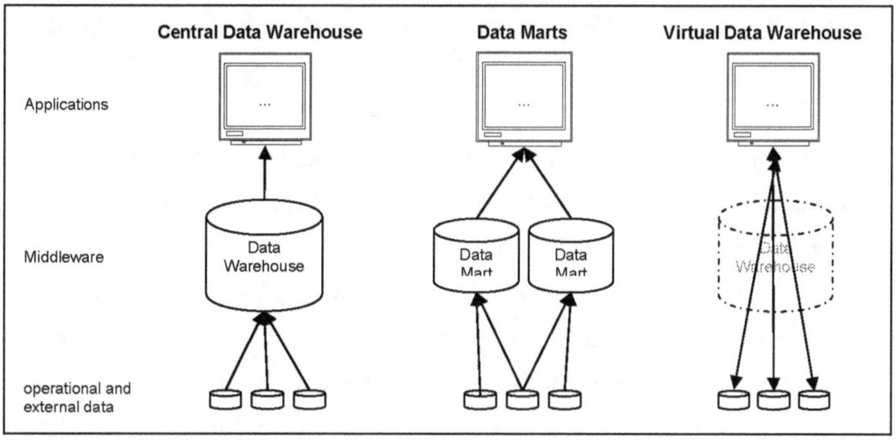

Source: Based on Bange, C. 2004, p. 71 and Gadatsch, A. 2005, p. 297 et seqq.

3.6   Data Synchronisation

The synchronisation of the DW with operational data and of DMs with the DW can be implemented in three different ways:[126]

1) Real-time/Event triggered update
2) Periodical update (batch)
3) Update based on the quantity of changes (message queue)

A *real-time update* is not only technologically difficult to implement, but also holds the danger in itself that the results of an analysis/a query are not duplicable as the data are constantly changing. The DW is populated with data when

---

[124] Cp.: ibid., Kemper, H.-G. et al. 2006, p. 35 et seqq.; Dippold, R. et al. 2005, p. 204 et seq.
[125] Cp.: Kemper, H.-G. et al. 2006, p. 36.
[126] Cp.: Kemper, H.-G. et al. 2006, p. 35.

the changing state of a data snapshot triggers the upload of this "new" data into the DW.[127] A better approach is a *periodical update*, for instance a daily batch run, to load data into the DW (and similar into the DMs). [128] This batch run can be conducted ideally at night when there is no other access to the DW or DM and the performance of the analytical applications is not critical.[129] An alternative approach is a *message queue* that receives the amount of changes made to operational data and stores the updated data until a defined amount of changes (for example: 1000 transactions) is reached (not depending of the period of time) and then triggers the ETL processes for the upload.[130]

Several authors postulate an even broadly accepted approach of joining the concepts of a central (core) DW and functional DMs in a complementing architecture.[131] The classical DW is used as the main storage (usually based on a RDBMS) and smaller DMs are populated with data by the means of additional ETL-processes from there.[132] Sometimes this architecture is supplemented by an ODS, i.e., a relational database with very low data latency for the purposes of ad-hoc-reporting on very recent data.[133] The concept of an ODS is tightly linked to the idea of real-time BI or at least right time BI as described before; the data in an ODS is much more recent than in a DW, but it might be difficult to reproduce the exact results of a query as the ODS might have been updated before. Therefore the much more stable data of the DW is of significant importance. Figure 9 on the next page illustrates this architecture.

While the analytical applications (such as OLAP or reporting tools) usually access data marts, the atomic data stored in the core DW are sometimes accessed by data mining applications for undirected analyses.

---

[127] Cp.: Inmon, W. H. 2005, p. 112 et seq.
[128] Cp.: Inmon, W. H. 2005, p. 106.
[129] Cp.: Ibid.
[130] Cp.: White, C. 22.01.2007, www.dmreview.com.
[131] Cp.: Kemper, H.-G. et al. 2006, p. 21; Inmon, W. H. et al. 2001, p. 13; Inmon, W. H. 2005, p. 3; Dippold, R. et al. 2005, p. 194 et seqq.; Knobloch, C. 2005, p. 53 et seq.; Bange, C. 2004, p. 80.
[132] Cp.: Inmon, W. H. 2005, p. 175. For a description of the ETL-processes refer to chapter 3.7.
[133] Cp.: Dippold, R. et al. 2005, p. 192 et seq.; Kemper, H.-G. et al. 2006, p. 21.

Figure 9: Central Data Warehouse <u>and</u> Data Marts Architecture

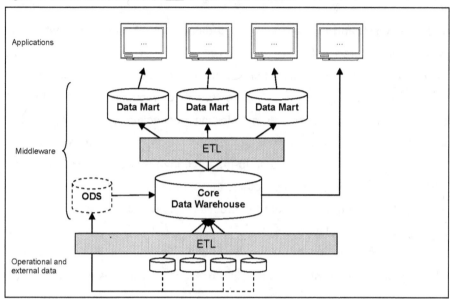

Source: Own presentation based on Kemper, H.-G. et al. 2006, p. 21 and Inmon, W. H. et al. 2001, p. 13

Table **4** conclusively summarises the main differences between data warehouses and data marts.

Table 4: Data Warehouse versus Data Mart

Characteristic	Data Warehouse	Data Mart
Managerial Objective	Efficient management support by the means of strategic, tactical, and operational information for all decision-maker in a company	Efficient decision support for one department, targeted at the requirements of analyses
Orientation	Company	Departments
Granularity of data	Atomic level of granularity	Aggregated data
Data Model	Relational → RDBMS	Multidimensional → MDBMS
Access	Usually no direct access by the average user, only for specific analyses by power users	Normally direct access by the user to the data mart possible
Degree of analysis's freedom	High degree of flexibility	Minor flexibility
Volume of data	More than 100 gigabyte to several terabyte	Several gigabyte to 100 gigabyte

Source: Adapted from Kemper, H.-G. et al. 2006, p. 36

3.7   Extraction, Transformation, Loading – Data Upload and Cleansing

The operational and transaction focused data of OLTP-applications which are collected and stored in the DW (and later also in the DMs) are characterised by a significant degree of heterogeneity (such as inconsistent structures, different 'names' for the same facts, etc.).[134] The process of populating data into the DW basically consists of the **extraction** (selection, connection, and conveyance into the staging area)[135] of data from OLTP-applications, the **transformation** of it (where necessary), and the actual up-**load** into the database.[136] As these processes are tightly linked to each other, the abbreviation **ETL** has been established in the literature[137] for both the processes as well as for applications (belonging to the this tool category).[138]

Planning and developing efficient ETL-processes in a data warehouse project is one of the most concerning problems (and might cause 80 % of the whole project budget) and therefore should be tackled very carefully.[139] Inmon gives multiple examples of the complexity of the process of transforming and loading data from operational sources into the analytical DW.[140]

The ETL-process generally consists of four phases, which are described in more detail below:[141]

- Filtering,
- Harmonisation,
- Aggregation, and
- Enrichment.

---

[134] Cp.: Kemper, H.-G./Finger, R. 2006, p. 114.
[135] Cp.: Bange, C. 2004, p. 87.
[136] Cp.: Bange, C. 2004, p. 74.
[137] Cp.: Knobloch, C. 2005, p. 52.
[138] Please refer to chapter 2.4 "Working Definition" for the distinction of "tool" and "application".
[139] Cp.: Bange, C. 2004, p. 86; Kemper, H.-G./Finger, R. 2006, p. 115; Böhnlein, M. et al. 2003, p. 177.
[140] Cp.: Inmon, W. H. 2005, p. 108 et seqq.
[141] Cp.: Kemper, H.-G. et al. 2006, p. 24.

3.7.1 Filtering

Filtering is the process of accessing data from the operational applications and cleansing it, i.e., correcting both syntactic as well as semantical failures.[142] Syntactic failures are related to the format and structure of the data whereas semantical ones are missing, inconsistent or outlier data values.[143] These corrections can either be executed automatically (for previously known and automatically recognisable failures) or manually (for those ones of a more complex structure).[144]

3.7.2 Harmonisation

An adequate filtering is a precondition for the process of *harmonisation*.[145] In this connexion the data's encodings (<u>different domains</u> for the same attribute's name and same semantical meaning), synonyms (<u>different attribute's name</u> for the same domain and same semantical meaning) and homonyms (same attribute's name for the same/different domains and <u>different semantical meaning</u>) are harmonised to facilitate a consistent interpretation of the stored information.[146] Additional differences between data from manifold operational databases can be different keys for the same subject (such as customer or product) and varying definitions of business terms or KPIs.[147]

3.7.3 Aggregation

Harmonised (and before filtered) data are summarised and accumulated values are calculated following predefined business rules during the process of *aggregation*. These procedures aim at an optimisation of the data warehouse's performance as calculated sums are stored as well to avoid a repeated calculation for each query which would deteriorate the response time.[148] Aggregated sums

---

[142] Cp.: Kemper, H.-G./Finger, R. 2006, p. 117 et seqq.
[143] Cp.: ibid., p. 220 et seq.
[144] Cp.: Kemper, H.-G. et al. 2006 p. 25 et seq.
[145] Cp.: Kemper, H.-G./Finger, R. 2006, p. 121 et seq.
[146] Cp.: ibid.; Inmon, W. H. et al. 2001, p. 70 et seqq.
[147] Cp.: Kemper, H.-G./Finger, R. 2006, p. 122.
[148] Cp.: Bange, C. 2004, p. 88.

are especially calculated for often used standardised reports and queries which are often used.[149]

3.7.4 Enrichment

Enrichment is the last step of ETL and is the augmentation of filtered, harmonised and aggregated data with functional aspects.[150] This functional context is reflected in the calculation of KPIs that are of significant relevance for several information demands such as variable costs or contribution margins.[151]

3.7.5 Closed-Loop Data Warehousing

Although the data upload from operational databases such as ERP-systems by the means of ETL is the standard way a DW (and from there DMs or other analytical tools) are populated, data might also externally be re-written into a DW. This happens especially in the process of planning and commenting;[152] therefore a DW always should include the possibility of manipulating and re-writing data from analytical applications. This concept is also called "closed-loop data warehousing" as the new data can immediately be used for efficient support of other decisions and analyses.[153]

3.8 Metadata Management

3.8.1 Definition and Importance

The common definition of metadata being "data about data"[154] is concretised in the context of BI and especially of a DW (as the main data management component of a BI-system) to be "everything about data needed to promote its administration and use".[155] Expressed in a more general way: metadata describe

---

[149] Cp.: Kemper, H.-G./Finger, R. 2006, p. 124 et seq.
[150] Cp.: ibid.
[151] Cp.: Bange, C. 2004, p. 86; Kemper, H.-G./Finger, R. 2006, p. 127.
[152] Cp.: Humm; B./Wietek, F. 2005, pp. 3 -14, here: p. 10; Inmon, W. H. et al. 2001, p. 23 et seq. (with several examples); Schinzer, H. et al. 1999, p. 93.
[153] Cp.: Kemper, H.-G. et al. 2006, p. 87.
[154] Cp. for example: Inmon, W. H. et al. 2001, p. 169; Dippold, R. et al. 2005, p. 98.
[155] Inmon, W. H. et al. 2001, p. 169.

the meaning and the characteristics of objects, i.e., data,[156] and are therefore a precondition for the communication of a DW's different components such as the ETL-layer and the core database.[157]

The importance of metadata in a DW is significantly higher than in the typical operational context,[158] especially due to the fact that by far more information have to be stored than in average OLTP-applications.[159] Metadata enable the user of a DW to navigate through its manifold possibilities, for instance by the means of presenting the different dimensions the analysts can select.[160] They describe not only the meaning and the structure of data in a DW but also their sources and their quality.[161] Therefore metadata deliver a structured, free-of-redundancy documentation of data and models for further processing.[162] A typical distinction made within metadata of a DW is the one between technical and semantical (or business) metadata.[163] The first ones are IT-orientated and are usually of importance for developers and administrators as well as they are tightly linked to the filtering process of ETL.[164] Semantical metadata, however, target at the meaning of and relationship between data stored in the DW: the user of the system is, for instance, informed about the calculation of KPIs or the data's sources.[165] These metadata are therefore linked to the stages of har-monisation, aggregation and enrichment during the ETL-process.[166]

A choice of concrete examples of metadata in a DW can be a lexicon of data terms used, a thesaurus of data objects, and a general documentation of the DW's tables.[167]

---

[156] Cp.: Kemper, H.-G. et al. 2006, p. 42.
[157] Cp.: Schinzer, H. et al. 1999, p. 25.
[158] Cp.: ibid.; Kemper, H.-G. et al. 2006, p. 47.
[159] Cp.: Kemper, H.-G. et al. 2006, p. 43.
[160] Cp.: Inmon, W. H. et al. 2001, p. 102 et seq.
[161] Cp.: Brunner, J./Dinter, B. 2003, p. 292.
[162] Cp.: Bange, C. 2004, p. 103.
[163] Cp.: Moss, L. T./Atre, S. 2003, p. 173; Bange, C. 2004, p. 105.
[164] Cp.: ibid. and Kemper, H.-G. et al. 2006, p. 44.
[165] Cp.: Bange, C. 2004, p. 105
[166] Cp.: Kemper, H.-G. et al. 2006, p. 44.
[167] Cp. with even more examples: Mucksch, H. 2006, p. 138 et seq.; Inmon, W. H. et al. 2001, p. 169 et seq.

3.8.2 Central versus Distributed Metadata Repository

Another aspect that has to be considered in the context of metadata is an architectural one. The metadata component of a DW can either be implemented as a centralised repository or several autonomous smaller repositories for each data warehouse's component.[168] The first approach offers one unified source of data definitions, structures, contents and use through the whole company.[169] The global access to all metadata and the avoidance of any exchange mechanisms such as interfaces are the advantages of this solution.[170] However, performance problems of large repositories and difficulties of a common understanding of business terms or KPIs[171] might lead to the implementation of decentralised autonomous metadata repositories. In that case, interfaces for the communication between these have to be developed and maintained.[172] Kemper and Inmon both propose a combination of these two approaches in order to find a balance with controlled redundancies but a substantiated common understanding throughout the company.[173]

---

[168] Cp.: Kemper, H.-G. et al. 2006, p. 46 et seqq. and Inmon, W. H. et al. 2001, p. 171 et seqq.
[169] Cp.: Inmon, W. H. et al. 2001, p. 171.
[170] Cp.: Kemper, H.-G. et al. 2006, p. 47.
[171] Cp.: Inmon, W. H. et al. 2001, p. 172.
[172] Cp.: Kemper, H.-G. et al. 2006, p. 47.
[173] Cp.: Kemper, H.-G. et al. 2006, p. 47 et seq.; Inmon, W. H. et al. 2001, p. 173 et seq.

4 Online Analytical Processing

Having established a qualitative and unified data basis within the data provision layer of Kemper's architectural framework[174] by the means of a DW, DMs and/or ODSs, the problem of transforming data into information and knowledge has to be tackled. This affects the middle layer of Kemper's framework (generation, storage and distribution of information).

In this chapter the basic form of analysing data (from a data warehouse or a data mart) is defined and introduced, i.e. online analytical processing (or abbreviated: OLAP). In the consecutive chapters the concepts of reporting and data mining as additional analytical as well as visualisation tools are presented.

4.1 Definition

The term OLAP was established in 1993 as a deliberate distinction from the known term of online transactional processing (OLTP).[175] It represents software technologies for dynamic and multidimensional analyses based on historic and consolidated company's data.[176] OLAP enables an ad-hoc explorative procedure where the user (or analyst) tries to evaluate the important aspects of a business problem following his own mental model.[177] At the beginning of an OLAP-analysis there is always a concrete business question to answer such as: "What was the revenue earned with product A sold to private customers in the 1st quarter in the region East?"[178] Deriving such information by the means of classical SQL-queries would be by far too slow and not interactive in the case that new questions might arise and would not support the analyst's speed of thought during the analysis.[179] The features of OLAP-analyses such as slice-and-dice or drill down, however, provide a company with the speed and analytical capabilities required.

---

[174] Cp.: chapter 2.5.3 "Layer Approach" and the previous chapter of this book.
[175] Cp.: Gluchowski, P./Chamoni, P. 2006, p. 145.
[176] Cp.: ibid. Therefore the ideal basis for OLAP-analyses is a data warehouse [annotation of the author].
[177] Cp.: Grothe, M./Gentsch, P. 2000, p. 58 et seq.
[178] Cp.: Kemper, H.-G. et al. 2006, p. 64 (adapted and translated by the author).
[179] Cp.: Grothe, M./Gentsch, P. 2000, p. 58 et seq.; Vitt, E. et al. 2002, p. 45.

4.2 Codd's Rules for Analytical Applications

Codd as one of the most important authors in respect of relational databases defined twelve rules that tools for adequate analytical processes should obey:[180]

1) Multidimensional conceptual views
2) Transparency
3) Possibility of access to relational and non-relational data sources
4) Stable response time
5) Client-server architecture
6) Generic dimensions (one logical structure for all dimensions)
7) Dynamic handling of sparsely populated matrices
8) Support of multi-user access
9) Unlimited operations through manifold dimensions
10) Intuitive data analysis and manipulation
11) Flexible reporting
12) Unlimited dimensions and aggregations

As these evaluation rules were developed with the support of a supplier of database technologies and were therefore very specific for one commercial purchasable product[181], they and the author's motivation have been consistently criticised.[182] Nevertheless this article was the first user orientated approach to the discussion on IT-based management support.[183]

Due to this criticism and an inflation of manifold additional (and also application focused) criteria for OLAP-tools[184], independent summarising rules evolved: the so called FASMI criteria that will be discussed in the next chapter.

---

[180] Cp. with more detailed explanations: Oehler, K. 2006, p. 8 et seqq.; Gluchowski, P./Chamoni, P. 2006, p. 146 et seqq.
[181] Cp.: Bange, C. 2004, p. 81.
[182] Cp.: Schinzer, H. et al. 1999, p. 43; Gluchowski, P./Chamoni, P. 2006, p. 146; Kemper, H.-G. et al. 2006, p. 94.
[183] Cp.: Kemper H.-G. et al. 2006, p. 94
[184] Cp.: Gluchowski, P./Chamoni, P. 2006, p. 149.

4.3 FASMI – Independent Requirements' Definition for OLAP

The acronym FASMI stands for **F**ast **A**nalysis of **S**hared **M**ultidimensional **I**nformation; these rules postulate a technologically and producer-independent catalogue of only five important requirements for tools that belong to the OLAP category. [185] Pendse and Creeth, the originators of this approach, reduced OLAP to five crucial points: speed, feasibility of analysis, security, multidimensionality, and adequate capacity. [186] These five criteria for the evaluation (and selection) of an OLAP-application reduce the amount of rules and are also neutral and not focusing on or promoting one specific application.

Table 5: FASMI Requirements

Requirement	Description
F(AST)	(Speed) – The average response time for queries should not be longer than five seconds; simple queries has to be answered within one second, more complex ones should not exceed 20 seconds of response time. The bottleneck are calculations that have to be made, not access to and presentation of the pure data.
A(NALYSIS)	(Feasibility) – The OLAP-application has to offer a broad range of analytical and statistical functionalities. That means that the user must be able to create new ad-hoc-queries and calculations without executing intensive programming.
S(HARED)	(Security) – A multi-user access must be possible. Basic (relational) databases' security functions (concurrent update locking, restore and backup) have to be provided.
M(ULTIDIMENSIONAL)	Multidimensionality is the essence of any OLAP-system. Data are provided within manifold dimensions including several hierarchies.[187]
I(NFORMATION)	(Capacity) – Objective of an OLAP analysis is gathering new information. Therefore the application must be able to store and maintain an adequate amount of data.

Source: Adapted from Nölken, D. 2002, p. 242 and Schinzer, H. et al. 1999, p. 45

4.4 Functionalities and Techniques

A multidimensional view on a company's data does not automatically require a physical multidimensional database, [188] as the star and the snowflake scheme also empower relational databases to represent multidimensional views on a set

---

[185] Cp. for example: ibid. and Grothe, M./Gentsch, P. 2000, p. 59.
[186] Cp.: Pendse, N./Creeth, R. 1995 in Schinzer, H. et al. 1999, p.45.
[187] Cp.: chapter 3.3 "Key Terms" and the there following chapters of this book for the definitions of hierarchies and dimensions.
[188] Cp.: Hannig, U. 2002, p. 11.

of data.[189] Depending on the database used as a source for the OLAP-application, a distinction can be made between relational OLAP (= ROLAP), multidimensional OLAP (= MOLAP), and a hybrid approach that tries to combine the advantages of each of the databases, i.e., hybrid OLAP (= HOLAP).[190] However, there are not any specific differences regarding the choice of basic technology, as the analytical techniques and functionalities are basically the same for all of these from a user perspective. As the advantages and disadvantages of RDBMS and MDBMS have been described before, the DBMS used must always fit the specific analytical purpose and situation of the company.

There are some basic techniques how a user can navigate through the multidimensional cubes of an OLAP application (which are in most cases based on a DW respectively on one of the DMs):[191]

- Slicing and Dicing,
- Rotating, and
- Drilling.

Slicing is the selection and analysis of a specific layer of a multidimensional data cube by keeping hold of one instance of one specific dimension. This process of filtering data by one instance of a dimension enables the user to reduce the amount of data and therefore to ease the analysis or to create reports answering very specific business problems.[192] **Dicing** cuts a smaller multidimensional cube out of and based on the dimensions of the original one.[193]

---

[189] Cp.: chapter 3.4 "Relational and Multidimensional Model" of this book [annotation of the author].
[190] Cp.: Schinzer, H. et al. 1999, p. 47 et seq.; Gluchowski, P./Chamoni, P. 2006, p. 155 et seqq.; Hannig, U. 2002 p. 12 et seqq. Other specialised occurrences of OLAP mentioned in this context are: DOLAP (desktop, independent from the company's network) and JOLAP (Java-based OLAP, metadata and OLAP data are administrated in a format not specific for any supplier, interface for Java 2 Enterprise Edition (J2EE)). However, some authors disapprove of such differentiations, cp. for example Grothe, M./Gentsch, P. 2000, p. 58 and Weber et al. 1999, p. 21.
[191] Please refer also to figure 10 at the end of this chapter (p. 38) for a graphical illustration of the different OLAP-techniques.
[192] Cp.: Nölken, D. 2002, p. 239; Oehler, K. 2006, p. 27; Bange, C. 2004, p. 96.
[193] Cp.: Kemper, H.-G. et al. 2006, p. 98.

Rotating is the process of swapping the logical axis of the cube, i.e. changing the order of the dimensions.[194] When the data cube is analysed as a cross-table (pivot-table), the swap of dimensions is the exchange of rows and columns. This change opens new perspectives of the same set of data for the analyst.

Drilling is the navigation in the data cube along the different instances of a dimension: it is following different levels of consolidation either from a summary figure down to finer sets of summarisations (drill-down) or vice versa from a detailed figure to an aggregated perspective (drill-up).[195] Doing this, the analyst can drill through the data down to the very reason of positive or negative variances in order to specify the real originates of outliers that he cannot recognise on an aggregated level.[196] The process of comparing different instances of one dimension on the same level of consolidation (such as the revenue of different stores in one country) is named drill-across.[197] As a "last consequence of drilling down"[198] the procedure of drilling-through from an aggregated view to one single transaction in order to check the basic data for the explanation of variances or outliers is ideally implemented in an OLAP-application. Such a drill-through usually leads to an operational database transaction but can also end at the atomic level of data in the DW.[199]

Of course it is not one single technique but the combination of these what supports the process of analyses at the speed of thought. Figure 10 below graphically summarises the different techniques.

---

[194] Cp.: Oehler, K. 2006, p. 27.
[195] Cp.: Inmon, W. H. 2005, p. 243; Nölken, D. 2002, p. 239; Hannig, U. 2002, p. 11.
[196] Cp. with an example: Nölken, D. 2002, p. 240 et seqq.
[197] Cp.: Bange, C. 2004, p. 96 et seq.
[198] Bange, C. 2004, p. 96.
[199] Cp.: ibid.; Oehler, K. 2006, p. 28.

Figure 10: OLAP Operations: Slicing, Dicing and, Drilling

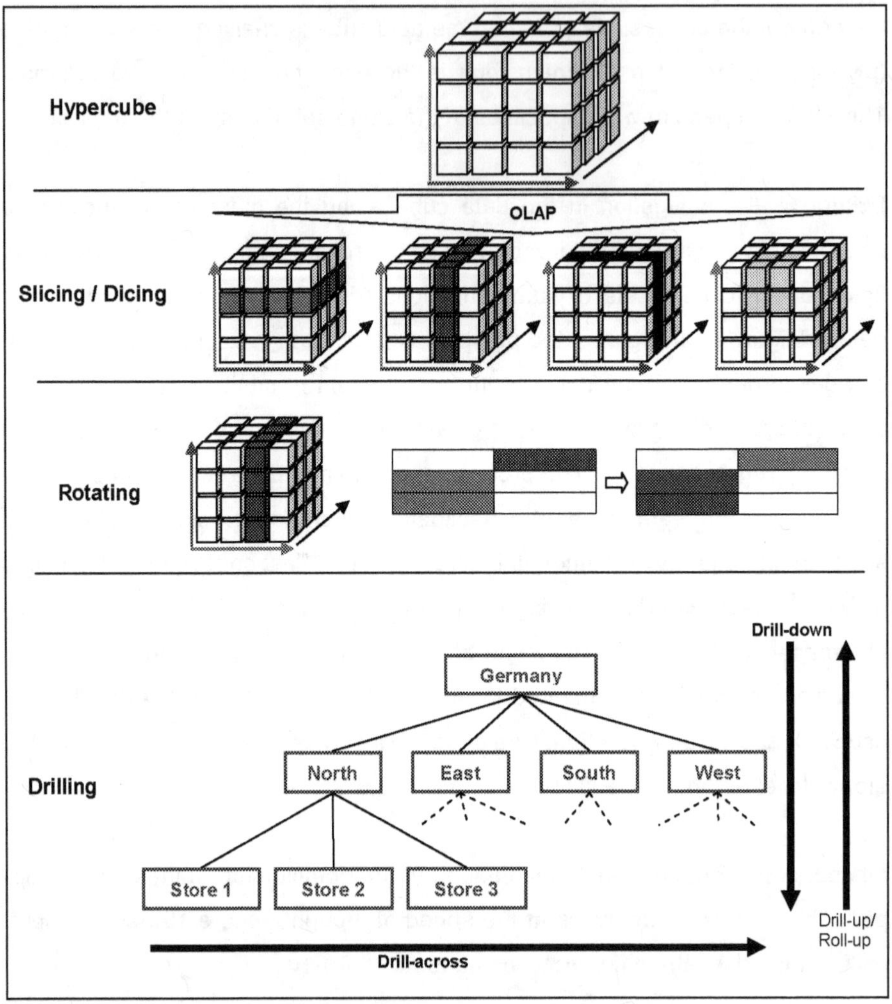

Source: Own presentation based on Hannig, U. 2002, p. 11; Bange, C. 2004, p. 96 and Schinzer, H. et al. 1999, p. 42

5 Reporting

According to Kemper a report is an overview of actual business facts regarding a defined area of responsibility in a prepared format.[200] The preparation can usually be seen in graphical visualisations in order to improve the ability of understanding for the recipients of the report.[201] A report in the context of BI therefore is a selected collection of data – most likely extracted from a DW/DM (or another data source) – presented in an easy understandable manner, i.e., tables, summaries, and graphical visualisation. Typically – and in a clear contrast to the OLAP process – there is no dynamic navigation in reports.[202]

It can be distinguished between active and passive reporting systems, differentiator for this is the actual trigger of the generation of the report.[203] OLAP ad-hoc analyses are classified as passive systems (as they do not provide any information without an user's input) and periodic (triggered usually by time) or aperiodic (but triggered without user input) reporting systems as being active ones.[204] Although OLAP-queries can be reasonably included into the generic term "reporting",[205] in this chapter only active (i.e., triggered) reporting systems are in focus.

5.1 Standard Reporting

The traditional active reporting is a *time period triggered* (that means for example a monthly) creation of predefined reports such as statutory external and (more often) internal financial statements.[206] This classical kind of reporting is also called *standard reporting*[207] and does not necessarily have to be a part of a BI-system as it could also receive data from operational (bookkeeping) systems. However, if a data warehouse or data marts exist in a company, it appears to be

---

[200] Cp.: Kemper, H.-G. et al. 2006, p. 110.
[201] Cp.: ibid.
[202] Cp.: Finger, R. 2002, p. 34.
[203] Cp.: Gluchowski, P. 1998, pp. 1174 – 1188, here: p. 1178 and Kemper, H.-G. et al. 2006, p. 111.
[204] Cp.: ibid.
[205] Cp.: Knobloch, C. 2005, p. 20.
[206] Cp.: Kemper, H.-G. et al. 2006, p. 111; Darpan, S. J. 2004, p. 104.
[207] Cp.: ibid.

logical to link the standard reporting (especially the internal) with this source of data. In general the requirements of the information demanders do not change very often.[208]

Predefined reports that are repetitively demanded for in non-periodical intervals and which are not triggered by events (so that these kind of reports do neither belong to the category of standard reporting nor to the one of exceptional reporting), can be stored in a reports' repository and then be retrieved by the user as required.[209]

5.2   Exceptional Reporting

Tighter embedded in a BI-system is an *event triggered reporting* or also called *exception reporting.*[210] Objective of this kind of reporting is to inform the company's management of significant variances or outliers in the set of data especially in between the dates of the regular (time triggered) creation of reports.[211] In order to implement such kind of automatic reporting, rules-based intelligent agents, i.e., monitoring applications enriched with workflow rules ("Who has to be informed in which case by which medium?"), are required.[212] Events to be observed by computerised agents (and which function then as a trigger) might be predefined limiting values of KPIs (as a calculated field value in a DW/DM) or also the availability of new data in the DW.[213] The question to consider is which KPIs to observe and which variances to set up as limiting values. Those questions can be answered best with some experience and historic values for the KPIs.

---

[208] Cp.: Bange, C. 2004, p. 94.
[209] Cp.: Finger, R. 2002, p. 34.
[210] Cp.: ibid. et seq.
[211] Cp.: Kemper, H.-G. et al. 2006, p. 112.
[212] Cp.: Bange, C. 2004, p. 95; Weber, J. et al. 1999, p. 37; Kemper, H.-G. et al. 2006, p. 112. Automated reports of this kind belong to the so called "push-concept" which will be introduced in more detail in chapter 7 "Knowledge Management" of this book.
[213] Cp.: Bange, C. 2004, p. 95; Kemper, H.-G. et al. 2006, p. 111. Of course the incidence of a specific date – such as the last day of a month – might be seen as an event as well (for example: Bange, C. 2004, p. 95). However, in this book such reports fall under the category of standard reporting (as they are time triggered) [annotation of the author].

The creation of such exceptional reports clearly aims at a reduction of decision (and action) latency: as earlier the management knows a fact as more efficiently adequate reactions can be initialised. [214] Of course the refresh period of the DW that is "observed" by intelligent agents is critical to the topicality of event triggered reports. The more a company comes closer to a real-time (or at least right-time) DW the higher are most-likely the benefits of those reports.[215]

5.3 Colour Coding

An often used technique of improving the explanatory power of a report (regardless whether it is a standard or an exceptional one) is the so-called "traffic lighting" or "colour coding".[216] This describes the conditional formatting (based on predefined rules) of figures, fields of a table, or parts of a graph in a report.[217] The coding with the typical colours of traffic lights (red, yellow, green) can help to lead the recipient of a report to the most important aspects; essential preconditions for an efficient leading are, however, well considered and reliable formatting rules. A problem to tackle, for instance, is a "normal" figure (no variances, ergo no coding) on an aggregated level but significant variances (and therefore colour coded values) on a disaggregated instance of this dimension. Although a "wrong" coding on the aggregated level might cause misinterpretation, the reader of the report has to find out about the variances and/or outliers on the more detailed level and therefore rules for a specialised coding or for automatically generated comments must be implemented in the agent program as well.[218]

---

[214] Cp.: chapter 2.6 "Real-Time Business Intelligence" of this book.
[215] Cp.: ibid.
[216] Cp.: Schinzer, H. et al. 1999, p. 75; Kemper, H.-G./Lee, P. 2002, p. 19.
[217] Cp.: ibid.
[218] Cp.: Schinzer, H. et al. 1999, p. 75 et seq.

6 Data Mining

Data Mining is the core of the knowledge discovery in databases (KDD) proc-ess,[219] which is the "organised process of identifying valid, novel, useful, and understandable patterns from large and complex data sets".[220] Data mining provides different computer automated exploratory methodologies for the dis-covery and interpretation of previously unknown patterns or relationships.[221] Data Mining has been developed from and influenced by several perspectives: basic principles come from statistics, machine learning, databases technolo-gies, algorithms, and information retrieval techniques.[222] Therefore manifold techniques and models exist belonging to data mining. The most important distinction between traditional multivariate statistics and data mining is that data mining techniques offer non-linear procedures of data analysis.[223]

Basis for all of these is the preparation of the data set to be explored; however, if data mining is based upon data from a DW, the quality of it is supposed to fit the purpose of data mining.[224]

Figure 11: Data Mining Methodologies

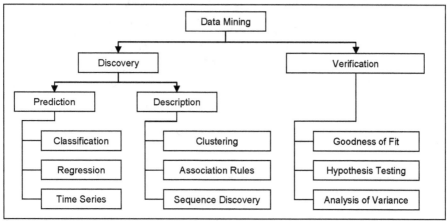

Source: Own presentation based on Dunham, M. H. 2003, p. 5; Maimon, O./Rokach, L. 2005a, p. 17.

---

[219] Cp.: Cios, K. J./Kurgan, L. A. 2005, p. 1.
[220] Maimon, O./Rokach, L. 2005a, p. 1.
[221] Cp.: Zaimer, A./Kashner, J. 2003, pp. 44 – 54, here: p. 54; Decker, R. 2003, p. 49.
[222] Cp.: Dunham, M. H. 2003, p. 12; Schinzer, H. et al. 1999, p. 100.
[223] Cp.: Otte, R. et al. 2004, p. 116.
[224] Cp.: Schinzer, H. et al. 1999, p. 103; Böhnlein, M. et al. 2003, p. 171 et seq.

Figure 11 above gives an overview on these different data mining methodologies, which will be presented in the course of this chapter. A first distinction is made between hypotheses triggered (directed) *verification* analyses (e.g., testing the goodness of a specific hypothesis) and undirected data-driven *discovery* analyses.[225] These can be further divided into predictive methodologies on the one hand and descriptive ones on the other hand.[226] While the latter ones describe a set of data by patterns found in itself, the first ones are used to predict unknown and future values of a given set of data variables (using known results found from different data).[227] In the following paragraphs these different techniques will be introduced.

6.1 Verification Techniques

Verification techniques are directed analyses because the analysts starts with a hypothesis that he wants to prove or disapprove. The source of this hypothesis is either an external – such as an expert – or an internal one, e.g., the analyst himself.[228] The techniques used for verification are common methods of traditional statistics: goodness of fit test, analysis of variances, and hypothesis testing.[229] Although there are authors who limit data mining only to discovery analyses,[230] this piece of work follows the opinion that the verification of the analyst's hypotheses is part of data mining methodologies, because data mining methodologies have been influenced by and still carry characteristics of manifold previously known techniques.

6.2 Predictive Techniques

The most common predictive techniques are classification, regression, and time series analysis.

---

[225] Cp.: Maimon, O./Rokach, L. 2005a, p. 6.
[226] Cp.: Dunham, M. H. 2003, p. 4.
[227] Cp.: Bange, C. 2004, p. 101; Maimon, O./Rokach, L. 2005a, p. 6 et seq.
[228] Cp.: Maimon, O./Rokach, L. 2005a, p. 7.
[229] Cp.: ibid.; Dunham, M. H. 2003, p. 54 et seq.
[230] Cp. for example: Böhnlein, M. et. al. 2003, p. 170.

6.2.1 Classification

Classification maps data objects into predefined groups or classes.[231] Starting with a set of example data a model is built reflecting the influence of an object's different attributes regarding its affiliation to one class.[232] Based upon this new data and objects can be automatically classified or predictions on unknown values of a given set of data can be made.[233] The classification model is usually created and trained in an iterative process in which an external instance (such as the analyst) assesses the quality of the classification in order to improve the quality of the model (supervised learning).[234] Methods used for classification are decision trees,[235] genetic algorithms, discriminant analysis, k-nearest-neighbours,[236] market basket analysis,[237] and neural networks.[238] These are on the one hand statistically based methods and on the other hand descending from the field of artificial intelligence.[239]

6.2.2 Regression

A *regression* model explains one dependent variable by the means of several independent variables; it is therefore used to explore an unknown characteristic (i.e., the value of the dependent variable) by the known values of the independent variables.[240] This data mining technique is used to develop typical predictive models, such as forecasting the long term demand for automotives or reconstructing time series.[241] Very complex models in time series prediction use not only the independent input variables but also the dependent (calculated) value of the preceding period (t-1) for the exploration of the next period's (t) value.[242] Methods utilised for regression are statistical ones (linear and multivariate re-

[231] Cp.: Dunham, M. H. 2003, p. 5; Bange, C. 2004, p. 102.
[232] Cp.: Bange, C. 2004, p. 102; Maimon, O./Rokach, L. 2005b, p. 149 et seq.
[233] Cp.: Schinzer, H. et al. 1999, p. 105.
[234] Cp.: ibid.
[235] Cp.: Dunham, M. H. 2003, p. 92 et seqq.
[236] Cp.: Dunham, M. H. 2003, p. 90 et seq.
[237] Cp. very detailed: Ghosh, J./Strehl, A. 2005, p. 75 et seqq.
[238] Cp.: Schinzer, H. et al. 1999, p. 107; Bange, C. 2004, p. 101.
[239] Cp.: Schinzer, H. et al. 1999, p. 106.
[240] Cp.: Beekmann, F./Chamoni, P. 2006, p. 265.
[241] Cp.: ibid.; Dunham, M. H. 2003, p. 5; Schinzer, H. et al. 1999, p. 105.
[242] Cp.: Beekmann, F./Chamoni, P. 2006, p. 265.

gression) as well as neural networks and machine learning (decision trees, genetic algorithms).[243]

6.2.3 Time Series Analysis

The last methodology used in the context of predictive analyses are traditional *time series analysis*: the variation of an attribute's value is examined over a specific period in regular points in time (such as minutes, hours, days, etc.).[244] This technique belongs to the area of classic statistics, but as it can be used as a preparatory analysis for the classification of the examined time line or for the prediction of future values based on the historic plot;[245] distance measures of different time lines can be used for examining their similarity.[246]

6.3 Descriptive Techniques

While the techniques described before always have a predictive element in their use, descriptive ones explore the properties of the set of examined data.[247] Techniques that are most commonly used for descriptive purposes are clustering, association rules, and sequence discovery.[248]

6.3.1 Clustering

Although *clustering* is similar to the technique of classification (and therefore to a predictive methodology),[249] it belongs to the descriptive techniques as it does not sort objects or predict their class, but rather explores segments (or cluster) in a given set of data.[250] The elements in each cluster are as similar as possible

---

[243] Cp.: Dunham, M. H. 2003, p. 5; Schinzer, H. et al. 1999, p. 106.
[244] Cp.: Dunham, M. H. 2003, p. 6.
[245] This is the technique of trend analysis [annotation of the author].
[246] Cp. with an example: Dunham, M. H. 2003, p. 6.
[247] Cp.: Dunham, M. H. 2003, p. 5.
[248] Cp.: ibid.; Maimon, O./Rokach, L. 2005a, p. 17. Dunham introduces also "summarisation" (also: characterisation, generalisation) as a descriptive data mining technique; however, as this method extracts or derives only representative information about the set of data to be examined (such as the mean of quantitative figures) and does not really explore unknown patterns, this book does not discuss this method in more detail; cp.: Dunham, M. H. 2003, p. 8 [annotation of the author].
[249] Cp.: chapter 6.2 „Predictive Techniques" of this book.
[250] Cp.: Dunham, M. H. 2003, p. 125.

on the one hand and the segments maximise the differences to each other on the other hand.[251] As a clustering model – in contrast to classification models – does not have to be trained before it can be used by the analyst, clustering methods are also referred to as unsupervised learning.[252] The discovery of cluster is the easier task, whereas the interpretation of the ones found is much more difficult.[253] Basis for establishing clusters is usually a similarity measure.[254] Within the methods for clustering models can be distinguished between hierarchical and partitional ones.[255] The first iterative ones can be either start from the bottom where each element is a single cluster and summarise these (agglomerative)[256] or with a single cluster (comprising all elements) which is divided (divisive method).[257] Partitional methods take the desired number of clusters as an input factor and creates only one set of clusters (and does not show the hierarchical composition of the clusters);[258] these are usually calculated by the k-means technique.[259] Another technique used for clustering is the construction of decision trees.[260] Clustering can be used preparatory to other data mining techniques in order to diminish the amount of data to be further analysed.[261]

6.3.2 Association Rules

Association rules (also link analysis) explore and explain regularities in the occurrences of different elements in data set records (or tuples of a relational database).[262] Rules describing the relationships between the different elements (items or values of an attribute) are the outcomes of an association analysis. An example for such a rule could be:

---

[251] Cp.: Schinzer, H. et al. 1999, p. 108; Beekmann, F./Chamoni, P. 2006, p. 265 et seq.
[252] Cp.: Dunham, M. H. 2003, p. 7.
[253] Cp.: Beekmann, F./Chamoni, P. 2006, p. 266.
[254] Cp.: Schinzer, H. et al. 1999, p. 108.
[255] Cp.: Dunham, M. H. 2003, p. 128.
[256] Cp.: Dunham, M. H. 2003, p. 132.
[257] Cp.: Schinzer, H. et al. 1999, p. 109; Beekmann, F./Chamoni, P. 2006, p. 274.
[258] Cp.: Dunham, M. H. 2003, p. 128.
[259] Cp.: Beekmann, F./Chamoni, P. 2006, p. 277 et seq.; Dunham, M. H. 2003, p. 140 et seqq.
[260] Cp.: Liu, B. et al. 2005, p. 99 et seqq.
[261] Cp.: Schinzer, H. et al. 1999, p. 104.
[262] Cp.: Bange, C. 2004, p. 103; Dunham, M. H. 2003, p. 8.

"If item A occurs in a tuple, then item B occurs there as well".[263]

The formal notation of the example rule is "A → B".[264] The quality of an association rule is measured by support (percentage of transactions in which that item/s
occur)[265] and confidence of strength (ratio of the number of transactions that
fulfil the rule A → B to the number of transactions that contain A).[266] The generation of rules can be constrained by the determination of minimum support
respectively confidence of strength in order to suppress irrelevant rules.[267]
There exist different algorithms for the extraction of rules from transactional
data: The most common and most recent one is the Apriori-algorithm;[268] prede-
cessors of this were for example the AIS-algorithm (Agrawal, Imielinski, Swami)
and the SETM (set-oriented mining for association rules).[269] One very important
aspect is to apply these algorithms to (relational) databases as they are often
used for data storage (such as in a DW).[270] Although the traditional application
of association rules is the analysis of market baskets, also other kinds of data
such as census data, linguistic data, insurance data, and medical diagnosis can
be analysed by the means of these algorithms.[271]

6.3.3 Sequence Discovery

Related to the analysis of association rules is the technique of *sequence discovery*. The distinctive character here is the element of time: associations are
not explored in one single transaction but rather in a time sequence (of actions).[272] A sequence pattern is therefore a homogeneous sequence of elements in different customers' transactions.[273] The items of a sequence (market
basket) analysis are not purchased at the same time but are purchased over

---

[263] Beekmann, F./Chamoni, P. 2006, p. 276 (translated by the author).
[264] Cp.: Höppner, F. 2005, p. 354.
[265] Cp.: Dunham, M. H. 2003, p. 165 et seq.
[266] Cp.: ibid.
[267] Cp.: Schinzer, H. et al. 1999, p. 120.
[268] Cp.: Dunham, M. H. 2003, p. 169 et seq.
[269] Cp.: Beekmann, F./Chamoni, P. 2006, p. 277 et seq.
[270] Cp.: Hipp, J. et al.2002, p. 28.
[271] Cp.: Höppner, F. 2005, p. 362.
[272] Cp.: Dunham, M. H. 2003, p. 9.
[273] Cp.: Schinzer, H. et al. 1999, p. 121.

time in a certain order.[274] The generation of sequence association rules can be constraint (as the simple association rules as well) by the determination of a minimum support or minimum confidence.[275] Sequence association rules belong to the area of temporal association rules;[276] an algorithm to identify frequent sequences is the SPADE (**S**equential **P**attern **D**iscovery using **E**quivalence classes) algorithm.[277] By the means of the knowledge about sequences in product sales more adequate and target-orientated advertising efforts can be undertaken to increase the selling of derived products.[278]

6.4 Recent Developments: Text and Web Mining

While the techniques all have been known for a longer period of time, the more recent developments in data mining are text and web mining techniques. Therefore these analyse typically unstructured data.[279]

Text mining is not only finding the best elements among a variety of documents, but also involves the discovery of previously unknown information in documents.[280] Implicit information are to be extracted from the texts analysed and presented to the reader.[281] Of relevance for managerial support are the following techniques:[282]

- Thematic indexation (identification of topics/themes),
- Segmentation (Clustering of texts with similar content),
- Classification (of texts and documents to predefined taxonomies), and
- Abstracting (automated summarisation and abstracting of texts).

Web mining is the mining of data related to the world wide web and can refer to the content, the HTML or XML code, the linkage structure between web pages,

---

[274] Cp.: Dunham, M. H. 2003, p. 9.
[275] Cp.: Schinzer, H. et al. 1999, p. 121.
[276] Cp.: Dunham, M. H. 2003, p. 9.
[277] Cp.: Dunham, M. H. 2003, pp. 262 and 271.
[278] Cp.: Beekmann, F./Chamoni, P. 2006, p. 278.
[279] Cp.: chapter 2.2 "Structure of Data" of this book.
[280] Cp.: Carpineto, C./Romano, G. 2004, p. 109.
[281] Cp.: Bange, C. 2004, p. 41.
[282] Cp.: ibid. p. 42 et seqq. with detailed explanations of these methods.

usage data, and user profiles.[283] As web mining is on the one hand applied to external web pages (such as the ones of competitors) but on the other hand on internal data (such as server log-files), this techniques in a away integrate both worlds.

Other recent developments in the area of data mining that shall be mentioned as short keywords are:

- XML (eXtended Query Language) as basis for storage and description of structured and semi-structured data and their relationships;[284]
- XRML (eXtended Rule Markup Language) as a language describing and processing rules implicit in web pages; it supports the convergence of artificial intelligence and knowledge management systems;[285]
- OLE DB-DM (Object Linking and Embedding Database for Data Mining) as an "extension of the SQL query language (...) to train and test data mining models".[286] It is used for the integration of data mining models with RDBMSs.[287]

The overall objectives are to integrate and semi-automate the processes of data mining and knowledge discovery regarding the manipulation and sharing of data as well as the development of data mining models.[288]

---

[283] Cp.: Dunham, M. H. 2003, p. 195. A complete taxonomy of web mining can be found at Srivastava, J. 2005, p. 276 [annotation of the author].
[284] Cp.: Cios, K. J./Kurgan, L. A. 2005, pp. 2 and 11.
[285] Cp.: Keyes, J. 2006, p. 152 et seq.
[286] Cios, K. J./Kurgan, L. A. 2005, p. 15.
[287] Cp.: Cios, K. J./Kurgan, L. A. 2005, p. 16.
[288] Cp.: ibid.

7 Knowledge Management

In this chapter the term knowledge management (KM) will be defined, techniques relevant in the context of BI are introduced and the concept of a BI focused portal as the single point of access to analyses, their outcomes, and additional information is evaluated.

7.1 Definition

According to Hannig KM is defined as a system of activities facilitating the utilisation of an organisation's knowledge by its members.[289] The main objectives of KM are as follows:[290]

- Recovery of knowledge from all available sources,
- Structuring, conditioning and storage of the generated knowledge, and
- Appropriate provision of knowledge.

Another aspect to consider is that a significant amount of knowledge is implicit knowledge, i.e., it is bound to a person and not explicitly stored as a document.[291] KM always has to target at the externalisation of this implicit knowledge in order to make an optimal use of the knowledge resource.[292]

There exist manifold techniques to promote the KM's objectives: on the one hand strategies for the transfer of existing knowledge within an organisation[293] as well as techniques for the engineering of new knowledge.[294] Due to the fact that not all of these are of significant relevance for the collaboration of BI and KM as will be introduced in the following chapters, only a few of those techniques are introduced in the following paragraphs.

---

[289] Cp.: Hannig, U. 2002, p. 16; similar Kemper, H.-G. et al. 2006, p. 128.
[290] Cp.: ibid. A summary of different other approaches to the definition of KM is offered by Dippold, R. et al. 2005, p. 259 et seqq.
[291] Cp.: Hannig, U. 2002, p. 16.
[292] Cp.: Hannig, U. 2002, p. 19.
[293] Cp.: Keyes, J. 2006, p. 22 et seqq.
[294] Cp.: Keyes, J. 2006, p. 45 et seqq.

7.2 Integration of Knowledge Management and Business Intelligence

Not only the management of BI-models and their outcomes (i.e., structured data)[295] but also of the integration of BI analyses with unstructured data (such as e-mails, minutes of meetings, notes, etc.) should be addressed in the context of the integration of KM and BI.[296] Three approaches can be identified for such an integration:[297]

1) Integration of BI- and KM-applications under one point of access
2) Utilisation of KM content within BI-processes
3) Distribution and utilisation of analyses and their outcomes by the means of KM

The first aspect aims at a web-based portal as the single point of access to both BI-applications and KM-tools. The characteristics of a portal and its benefits will be discussed in more depth in the following chapter.

The utilisation of KM content within BI-processes is also proposed by Bange who introduces the concept of document warehousing as a complementary addition to the traditional data warehouse.[298] The essential distinction between a document management system (DMS)[299] as a traditional KM-tool and a document warehouse is the semantical enrichment of documents stored in it by the means of indexation, segmentation, classification, and abstraction.[300] These new generated metadata then can be used in the process of information retrieval (i.e., the "representation, organisation, storage of; and access to information").[301] Based on this concept the presentation of KPIs in a MIS/EIS, for in-

---

[295] Cp.: Kemper, H.-G. et al. 2006, p. 128.
[296] Cp.: Bange, C. 2004, p. 116 et seqq.
[297] Cp.: Kemper, H.-G./Baars, H. 2005, p. 120 et seq.
[298] Cp.: ibid.
[299] A DMS systematically administrates and centrally stores all computer generated or even imaged documents (Cp.: Hannig, U. 2002, p. 22 et seq.) [annotation of the author].
[300] Cp.: Bange, C. 2004, p. 117 and chapter 6.4 "Recent Developments: Text and Web Mining" of this book [annotation of the author].
[301] Bange, C. 2004, p. 20.

stance, can be augmented by the automated allocation of content matching documents.[302]

The last aspect is also mentioned and evaluated by Kemper.[303] The storage of BI-analysis models and the outcomes should be supported by well-defined processes as well as a content management system (CMS). A CMS adminis-trates media content (such as numeric data, texts, graphics, pictures, audio files, and video sequences)[304] and aims at the generation, control, releasing, and publication of contents in the inter-, intra and extranet.[305] Therefore it is a crucial precondition for the distribution of knowledge generated within the BI-process by the means of the intranet.

7.3 Business Intelligence Portal

The general definition of a portal being "a web-based, personalised central point of access to applications and information"[306] has to be specified for the pur-poses of a business intelligence portal. Therefore a categorisation of portals is introduced and the different functionalities of a BI-portal areevaluated.

Figure 12: Classes of Portals

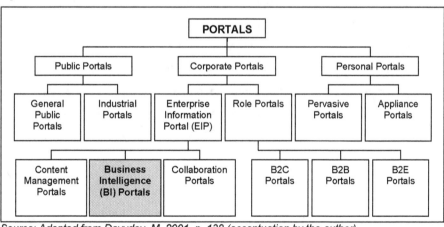

Source: Adapted from Davydov, M. 2001, p. 138 (accentuation by the author)

---

[302] Cp.: Bange, C. 2004, p. 103.
[303] Cp.: Kemper, H.-G. et al. 2006, p. 128.
[304] Cp.: Kemper, H.-G. et al. 2006, p. 129.
[305] Cp.: Hannig, U. 2002, p. 23.
[306] Bange, C. 2004, p. 144.

A broadly accepted classification of portals is proposed by Davydov and depicted in figure 12 on the previous page.[307] Therefore a business intelligence portal belongs to the category of enterprise information portals. The categories as illustrated in this figure are of a more theoretical importance as there cannot be made such sharp distinctions between the different kind of portals in practice.

According to the layer approach by Kemper a BI-portal ideally is the access tier to information and knowledge that has been generated within the BI-system.[308] As a single point of access it subsumes different front-end-tools of the BI-system. The differentiations between the three sub-categories of EIPs (Content Management Portal, Collaboration Portal, and BI Portal) are of a more theoretical nature and become blurred more and more as an integration and consolidation to all-embracing portals can be recognised.[309]

7.3.1 Principals of Push and Pull

The objectives of a better support of the user within the process of analyses and especially the improvement of the communication of findings by the means of the BI-portal can be further supported by either push- or pull-models for the distribution of information and reports.[310] The pure form of the push-model is the distribution of any new report or analysis to every member of an organisation: this would end up in a situation of an "information overload".[311] The extreme opposite would be only providing information in a specified source (such as a BI/KM database) and the (potential) recipients being responsible for pulling the information.[312] A danger in this case is – in contrast to the push-model – that

---

[307] Davydov, M. 2001, p. 138; cited for instance by: Bange, C. 2004, p. 145; Kemper, H.-G. et al. 2006, p. 133. Due to the fact that not all of those portals can be discussed here in detail please refer for detailed explanations of the different portals to the sources mentioned here.
[308] Cp.: Kemper, H.-G. et al. 2006, p. 11 and chapter 2.5.3 "Layer Approach" of this book.
[309] Cp.: Kemper, H.-G. et al. 2006, p. 134.
[310] Cp.: Gehra, B. et al. 2005, pp. 236-242, here: p. 236.
[311] Cp.: Grothe, M./Gentsch, P. 2000, p. 255.
[312] Cp.: ibid.

important facts are not recognised by the adequate and responsible employees.[313] Figure 13 below illustrates these two antithetic principles.

Figure 13: Principals of Push and Pull

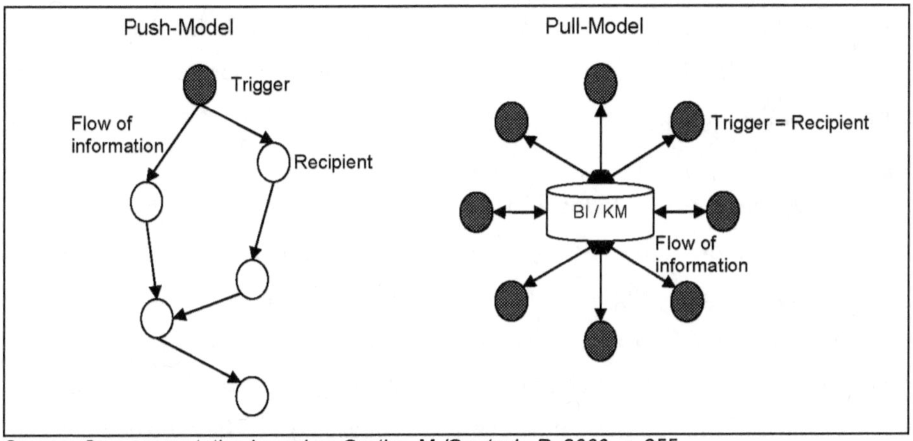

Source: Own presentation based on Grothe, M./Gentsch, P. 2000, p. 255.

A combination of both principles, however, appears to be more promising: In a profile of interest can every employee define his areas of interest (pull) but in addition he is also provided with adequate information depending on his role (push).[314]

7.3.2 Advantages of a Business Intelligence Portal

As a portal is a web-based application, it is operating in a browser and the local installation of applications on the user's computer can be reduced by central (server-based) applications.[315] Front-end tools for the access to analytical tools or for the presentation of analyses' findings do not have to be installed on each client but are operated and maintained on a server and accessed via the BI-portal.

A BI-portal is not only meant to function as a single point of access but also to offer easy understandable overviews on the company's current situation. There-

---

[313] Cp.: ibid.
[314] Cp.: Grothe, M./Gentsch, P. 2000, p. 256.
[315] Cp.: Bange, C. 2004, p. 144.

fore techniques of visualisation and presentation of data and analyses are of significant importance in this context. Not only the broadly known and used standard visualisation functionalities of MS Excel can be used for improving the perceivability of pure facts and figures[316] but also very sophisticated techniques of presentation such as scattergrams, trajectory graphs, kiviat diagrams, and even geographical maps enriched with business information support the easiness of understanding.[317]

An analyst has the knowledge and the ability to create and navigate through ad-hoc-reports whereas a member of the executive management requires aggregated and at a glance understandable reports.[318] For those the BI-portal might be reduced to a MIS/EIS presenting first and foremost information and not being so much point of access to the analytical tools. One approach to this problem is the creation of management dashboards (or cockpits).[319] They provide the user – just like a dashboard in a car – within a short glance with the most important information of the company's situation. Therefore the visualisation of adequate KPIs is to address for each user of such a management dashboard.[320]

---

[316] Cp.: Schinzer, H. et al. 1999, p. 72.
[317] Cp. with examples: Dull, R. B./Tegarden, D. P. 2004, p. 161 et seqq.; Schinzer, H. et al 1999, p. 73 et seq.
[318] Cp.: Bange, C. 2004, p. 93.
[319] Cp.: ibid.
[320] Cp.: ibid.

8   Users of Business Intelligence

The users of BI-systems can be categorised and should be individually addressed in order to maximise their personal and the company's benefits of the
information and knowledge generated.

One approach by Vitt is a pyramidal division into information users at the bottom, information consumers in the middle layer and power analysts at the
top.[321] The biggest group of *information users* require standardised and structured reports and no capability to perform OLAP-analyses.[322] The *information
consumer* in contrast requires the ability (and also has the capability) to perform
guided dynamic queries and ad-hoc reporting; however he is not an expert of
database design and query tools.[323] The *power analyst* at the top of the pyramid
has the ability and knowledge to make full use of the BI-system's capabilities;
this is usually the smallest group of users.[324]

Figure 14: Business Intelligence User Communities by Vitt and Kemper

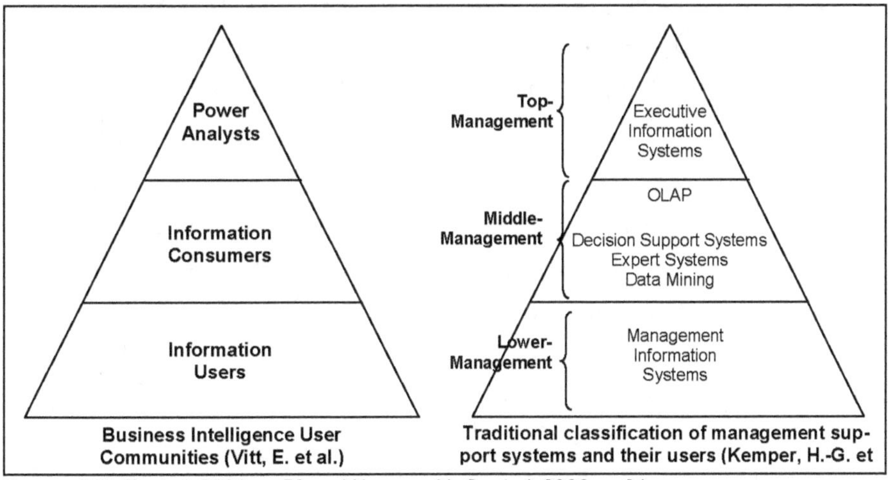

Source: Vitt, E. et al. 2002, p. 56 and Kemper, H.-G. et al. 2006, p. 81

However, this pyramidal approach (by Vitt et al.) is only focused on the number
of users in a group and this depiction must not be confused with the traditional

---

[321] Cp.: Vitt, E. et al. 2002, p. 54 et seqq.
[322] Cp.: Vitt, E. et al. 2002, p. 55.
[323] Cp.: Vitt, E. et al. 2002, p. 56.
[324] Cp.: ibid.

hierarchical one with the executive management at the top of the pyramid, presented for instance by Kemper.[325] A member of the top-management is more likely a information user than a power analyst. Kemper himself criticises his (former) classification of management support systems due to the fact that there are practically not such clear distinctions between the different classes of systems as theoretically proposed and even the allocation of hierarchies to these classes is obsolete in the context of state-of the art analytical (BI-)systems.[326]

Another quite picturing approach to describe user groups of a BI-system is made by Inmon who distinguishes between

- Tourists,
- Farmers,
- Explorers, and
- (Data) Miners.[327]

Tourists have a breadth of knowledge instead of a depth. They know where to find information, interpret and make use of metadata and understands the structure of a BI-system.[328] As they do not really know the requirements of a specific analysis, they make use of manifold applications of the BI-system and sometimes find interesting arenas for further analysis.[329] Although they have some characteristics of power analysts, they cannot be totally compared to those as tourists stroll through data that might be of interest more by chance than based with a specific analytical purpose.

A *farmer* is very predictable in his use of the BI-applications. He usually does the same activities on a regular basis, such as processing predefined que-

---

[325] Kemper, H.-G. et al. 2006, p. 81.
[326] Cp.: ibid.
[327] Cp.: Inmon, W. H. 2005 p. 457 et seqq. and Inmon, W. H. et al. 2001, p. 30 et seq. An overview illustrating the areas of analyses for all of these user groups can be found at Inmon, W. H. et al. 2001, p. 36.
[328] Cp.: Inmon, W. H. 2005 p. 459 and Inmon, W. H. et al. 2001, p. 32.
[329] Cp.: ibid.

ries.[330] They are typical "information users" and therefore access small amounts of data, often in data marts.

Explorers operate the BI-applications with a high degree of unpredictability and irregularity and often access massive amounts of data while processing their analyses.[331] As he does not know the next steps of his analysis at the beginning of it, his explorations of data can be called to be heuristic.[332] The outcomes of his analyses are assertions and hypotheses. He can be considered to be (in a way a part of) a power analyst.

The *(data) miner* (representing the missing characteristics of the power analyst) processes data mining analyses of all kinds especially verification analyses.[333] He has special mathematical and statistical skills and operates in strong rela-tionship with the explorer: The explorer discover a hypothesis which is then proved or disapproved by the miner.[334] As he looks over many rows of data while processing his mining activities the size of his queries might be very large.[335]

[330] Cp.: Inmon, W. H. 2005 p. 458 and Inmon, W. H. et al. 2001, p. 33.
[331] Cp.: ibid.
[332] Cp.: ibid.
[333] Cp.: Inmon, W. H. 2005, p. 459 and Inmon, W. H. et al. 2001, p. 34 et seq.
[334] Cp.: Inmon, W. H. 2005, p. 459 and Inmon, W. H. et al. 2001, p. 35.
[335] Cp.: ibid.

9 Resume

Companies are required to forecast their financial situation as accurate as possible in order to allocate their financial resources in an optimised manner. The computer-based support of forecasting processes within a company has fast developed in the past few decades. One of the most recent developments since the middle of the 1990s can be subsumed under the term "Business Intelligence".

BI is the process of transforming data which exist in an enterprise into information and then into knowledge and hopefully into intelligence. This process is supported by different tools as introduced in this book:

- Data Warehouse/Data Marts,
- Extraction, Transformation, Loading,
- Online Analytical Processing,
- Reporting, and
- Data Mining.

Data warehouses and data marts collect and provide data of high quality for further analysis; the population of these is conducted through very complex ETL-processes. OLAP, reporting and data mining are analytical tools which transform data into new information. Qualified users of those tools might then be able to gain new knowledge and intelligence from these information. There are also important interfaces between business intelligence and Knowledge management. The knowledge generated by the means of BI has to be distributed as well as information provided by classical KM tools might be utilised in BI processes. A BI portal (or at least of a business intelligence component of an existing corporate intranet portal) joins aspects of BI and KM. These BI-tools usually are embedded in a complex system of different applications and not used as stand-alone solutions.

List of References

Monographs and Collected Editions

Anandarajan, A. et al.: Historical overview of Accounting Information Systems, in: Anandarajan, M. et al. (editors): Business Intelligence Techniques: a Perspective from Accounting and Finance; Berlin et al., 2004, pp. 1-20

Bange, C.: Business Intelligence aus Kennzahlen und Dokumenten – Integration strukturierter und unstrukturierter Daten in entscheidungsunterstützenden Informationssystemen, Hamburg, 2004. Zugl.: Dissertation, Universität Würzburg, 2003

Beekmann, F./Chamoni, P.: Verfahren des Data Mining, in: Chamoni, P./Gluchowski, P. (Hrsg.): Analytische Informationssysteme – Business Intelligence-Technologien und -Anwendungen, 3. Aufl., Berlin/Heidelberg, 2006, S. 263-282

Böhnlein, M. et al.: Synergieeffekte zwischen Data Warehousing, OLAP und Data Mining – eine Bestandsaufnahme, in: von Maur, E./Winter, R. (Hrsg.), Data Warehouse Management – Das St. Galler Konzept zur ganzheitlichen Gestaltung der Informationslogistik, Berlin et al., 2003, S. 167-193

Brunner, J./Dinter, B.: Vom Data Warehouse zum Business Performance Measurement – Anforderungen an das Metadatenmanagement, in: von Maur, E./Winter, R. (Hrsg.), Data Warehouse Management – Das St. Galler Konzept zur ganzheitlichen Gestaltung der Informationslogistik, Berlin et al., 2003, S. 291-311

Carpineto, C./Romano, G.: Concept Data Analysis – Theory and Applications, Chichester, 2004

Cios, K. J./Kurgan, L. A.: Trends in Data Mining and Knowledge Discovery, in: Pal, N. R./Jain, L. (editors): Advanced Techniques in Data Mining and Knowledge Discovery, London, 2005, pp. 1-26

Darpan, S. J.: Online Analytical Processing in Accounting, in: Anandarajan, M. et al. (editors): Business Intelligence Techniques: a Perspective from Accounting and Finance; Berlin et al., 2004, pp. 93-116

Davydov, M.: Corporate Portals and e-Business Integration, New York, 2001.

Decker, R.: Data Mining und Datenexploration in der Betriebswirtschaft, in: Schwaiger, M./Harhoff, D. (Hrsg.): Empirie und Betriebswirtschaft, Stuttgart, 2003, S. 47-82

Devine, P. W. et al.: Importance of Data in Decision-Making, in: Anandarajan, M. et al. (ed.): Business Intelligence Techniques: a Perspective from Accounting and Finance; Berlin et al., 2004, pp. 21-39

Dippold, R. et al.: Unternehmensweites Datenmanagement – Von der Datenbankadministration bis zum Informationsmanagement, 4. überarb. u. erw. Aufl., Wiesbaden, 2005

Dittmar, C./Gluchowski, P.: Synergiepotenziale und Herausforderungen von Knowledge Management und Business Intelligence, in: Hannig, U. (Hrsg.): Knowledge Management und Business Intelligence, Berlin et al., 2002, pp. 27-41

Dull, R. B./Tegarden, D. P.: Visual Representations of Accounting Information, in: Anandarajan, M. et al. (ed.): Business Intelligence Techniques: a Perspective from Accounting and Finance; Berlin et al., 2004, pp. 149-166

Dunham, M. H.: Data Mining: Introductory and Advanced Topics, Upper Saddle River, 2003

Finger, R.: Unternehmensweite Data Warehouses – Machbar oder Mythos?, in: Kemper, H.-G./Mayer, R. (Hrsg.): Business Intelligence in der Praxis: Erfolgreiche Lösungen für Controlling, Vertrieb und Marketing, Bonn, 2002, S. 29-43

Ford Motor Company: Ford Motor Company 2005 Annual Report – Driving Innovation, Dearborn, 2006

Gadatsch, A.: Grundkurs Prozessmanagement, 4. erw. Aufl., Wiesbaden, 2005

Ghosh, J./Strehl, A.: Clustering and Visualization of retail Market Baskets, in: Pal, N. R./Jain, L. (editors): Advanced Techniques in Data Mining and Knowledge Discovery, London, 2005, pp. 75-102

Gluchowski, P./Chamoni, P.: Entwicklungslinien und Architekturkonzepte des OLAP, in: Chamoni, P./Gluchowski, P. (Hrsg.): Analytische Informationssysteme – Business Intelligence-Technologien und –Anwendungen, 3. Aufl., Berlin/Heidelberg, 2006, S. 143-176

Grothe, M./Gentsch, P.: Business Intelligence – Aus Informationen Wettbewerbsvorteile gewinnen, München et al., 2000

Hannig, U.: Knowledge Management + Business Intelligence = Decision Intelligence, in: Hannig, U. (Hrsg.): Knowledge Management und Business Intelligence, Berlin et al., 2002, pp. 3-26

Hipp, J. et al.: Data Mining of Association Rules and the Process of Knowledge Discovery in Databases, in: Perner, P. (Hrsg.): Advances in Data Mining – Applications in E-Commerce, Medicine and Knowledge Management, Berlin et al., 2002, S. 15-36

Höppner, F.: Association Rules, in: Maimon, O./Rokach, L. (editors): The Data Mining and Knowledge Discovery Handbook, New York et al., 2005, pp. 353-376

Inmon, W. H.: Building the Data Warehouse, 4th ed., Indianapolis, 2005

Inmon, W. H. et al.: Corporate Information Factory, 2nd ed., New York et al., 2001

Kemper, A./Eickler, A.: Datenbanksysteme – Eine Einführung, München/Wien, 2006

Kemper, H.-G./Baars, H.: Integration von Wissensmanagement- und "Business Intelligence"-Systemen – Potenziale, in: Foschani, S. (Hrsg.): Strategisches Wertschöpfungsmanagement in dynamischer Umwelt : Festschrift für Erich Zahn, Frankfurt a. Main, 2005, S. 117-137

Kemper, H.-G./Finger, R.: Transformation operativer Daten: Konzeptionelle Überlegungen zur Filterung, Harmonisierung, Aggregation und Anreicherung im Data Warehouse, in: Chamoni, P./Gluchowski, P. (Hrsg.): Analytische Informationssysteme – Business Intelligence-Technologien und –Anwendungen, 3. Aufl., Berlin/Heidelberg, 2006, S. 113-128

Kemper, H.-G./Lee, P.: Business Intelligence (BI) – Innovative Ansätze zur Unterstützung der betrieblichen Entscheidungsfindung, in: Kemper, H.-G./Mayer, R. (Hrsg.): Business Intelligence in der Praxis: Erfolgreiche Lösungen für Controlling, Vertrieb und Marketing, Bonn, 2002, S. 11-29

Kemper, H.-G. et al.: Business Intelligence – Grundlagen und praktische Anwendungen: Eine Einführung in die IT-basierte Managementunterstützung, 2. erg. Aufl., Wiesbaden, 2006

Keyes, J.: Knowledge Management, Business Intelligence, and Content Management: The IT Practitioner's Guide, Boca Raton/New York, 2006

Knobloch, C.: Business Intelligence-Komponenten – Theorie, Realisierung, Entwicklungsprozess, Herdecke/Bochum, 2005

Liu, B. et al.: Clustering via Decision Tree Construction, in: Chu, W./Lin, T. S. (editors): Foundations and Advances in Data Mining, Berlin et al., 2005, pp. 99-124

Maimon, O./Rokach, L.: Introduction to Knowledge Discovery in Databases, in: Maimon, O./Rokach, L. (editors): The Data Mining and Knowledge Discovery Handbook, New York et al., 2005, pp. 1-17 (2005a)

Maimon, O./Rokach, L.: Introduction to Supervised Models, in: Maimon, O./Rokach, L. (editors): The Data Mining and Knowledge Discovery Handbook, New York et al., 2005, pp. 149-164 (2005b)

Moss, L. T./Atre, S.: Business Intelligence Roadmap: The complete Lifecycle for Decision-Support Applications, Boston et al., 2003

Mucksch, H.: Das Data Warehouse als Datenbasis analytischer Informations-systeme, Chamoni, P./Gluchowski, P. (Hrsg.): Analytische Informationssysteme – Business Intelligence-Technologien und –Anwendungen, 3. Aufl., Ber-lin/Heidelberg, 2006, S. 129-142

Nölken, D.: Controlling mit Intranet- und Business Intelligence Lösungen, Frankfurt am Main et al., 2002. Zugleich: Universität Dortmund, Dissertation 2000

Oehler, K.: Corporate Performance Measurement mit Business Intelligence Werkzeugen, München/Wien, 2006

Otte, R. et al.: Data Mining für die industrielle Praxis, München/Wien, 2004

Perridon, L./Steiner, M.: Finanzwirtschaft der Unternehmung, 14. überarb. Aufl., München, 2007

Schinzer, H. et al.: Data Warehouse and Data Mining: Marktführende Produkte im Vergleich, 2. völlig überarb. Aufl., München, 1999

Srivastava, J. et al.: Web Mining – Concepts, Applications and Research Di-rections, in: Chu, W./Lin, T. S. (editors): Foundations and Advances in Data Mining, Berlin et al., 2005, pp. 275-307

Vitt, E. et al.: Business Intelligence: Making better Decisions faster, Redmond, 2002

Weber, J. et al.: Business Intelligence, Vallendar, 1999

Articles in Periodicals/Scientific Journals

Auer, U.: Die Jetzt-Wirtschaft wartet nicht: mit Business Intelligence zum Echt-zeitunternehmen, in: Computerwoche, 31. Jg. (2004), Heft 9, S. 34-35

Codd, E.: A Relational Model for Large Shared Data Banks, in: Communications of the ACM, Vol. 13 (1970), No. 6, pp. 377-387

Gehra, B. et al.: Business Intelligence for the Masses: Datenaufbereitung und Datenanalyse für den Controller im Wandel, in: Zeitschrift für Controlling und Management, 49. Jg. (2005), Heft 3, S. 236-242

Gluchowski, P.: Werkzeuge zur Implementierung des betrieblichen Berichts-wesens, in WISU, 27. Jg. (1998), Heft 10, S. 1174-1188

Humm, B./Wietek, F.: Architektur von Data Warehouses und Business Intelligence Systemen, in: Informatik Spektrum, 28. Jg. (Feb. 2005), Heft 1, S. 3–14

Klaus, A.: Die Business Intelligence Megatrends – The Future starts Now, in: Geldinstitute, 37. Jg. (2006), Heft 5, S. 26-27

Maluf, D. et al.: Business Intelligence in large Organizations: Integrating which data?, in: Lecture notes in Computer Science, w/o Vol. (2006), No. 4203, pp. 248-257

Pendse, N./Creeth, R.: The OLAP-Report: Succeeding with On-Line Analytical processing, Vol. 1, Business Intelligence, without location, 1995

Whiting, R.: Crystal-Ball Glance into Fiscal Future – Forecasting software offers better accuracy of profit-and-loss management, in: Informationweek, Vol. 14 (22. July 2002), p. 37

Internet Sources (world-wide web)

Blumberg, R./Atre, S.: The Problem with Unstructured Data, in: DM Review Magazine, Vol. 13 (Feb. 2003), http://www.dmreview.com/article_sub.cfm?articleId=6287, [12.03.2007]

Inmon, W. H.: The Government Information Factory and the Zachman Framework, January 2003, http://www.teradata.com/t/pdf.aspx?a=134008&b=133955, [22.01.2007]

White, C.: Now is the right Time for Real-Time BI, in: DM Review Magazine, Vol. 14 (Sep. 2004), No. 9, http://www.teradata.com/t/pdf.aspx?a=134008&b=133985, [22.01.2007]

Zachman Institute for Framework Advancement (ZIFA): Enterprise Architecture: A Framework (Zachman Framework – Framework Overview), http://zifa.com/framework.pdf, [28.01.2007]

Bibliography/Further Reading

Monographs and collected editions

Aranze, B./Amobi, O.: A Methodology for developing Business Intelligence Systems, in: Anandarajan, M. et al. (editors): Business Intelligence Techniques: a Perspective from Accounting and Finance; Berlin et al., 2004, pp. 181-195

Giudici, P.: Applied Data Mining: Statistical Methods for Business and Industry, Chichester, 2003

Hastie, T. et al.: The Elements of Statistical Learning – Data Mining, Inference and Prediction, New York et al., 2001

Jhaveri, D. S.: Online Analytical Processing in Accounting, in: Anandarajan, M. et al. (editors): Business Intelligence Techniques: a Perspective from Accounting and Finance; Berlin et al., 2004, pp. 93-115

Kovalerchuk, B./Vityaev, E.: Data Mining for Financial Applications, in: Maimon, O./Rokach, L. (editors): The Data Mining and Knowledge Discovery Handbook, New York et al., 2005, pp. 1204-1224

Makridakis, S. et al.: Forecasting: Methods and Applications, 3rd ed., New York et al., 1998

Articles

Bange, C.: Werkzeuge für Business Intelligence, in: Heilmann, H. et al. (Hrsg.): HMD – Praxis der Wirtschaftsinformatik: Business & Competitive Intelligence, o. Jg. (Februar 2006), Heft 247, S. 63-73

Chamoni, P./Gluchowski, P.: Integrationstrends bei Business-Intelligence-Systemen: Empirische Untersuchung auf Basis des Business Intelligence Maturity Model, in: Wirtschaftsinformatik, 46. Jg. (2004), Heft 2, S. 119-128

Chen, J.-S./Lin, P.-L.: An intelligent Financial Ratio Selection Mechanism for Earning Forecast, in: Journal of the Operations Research Society of Japan, Vol. 45 (Dec. 2002), No. 4, pp. 373-384

Gluchowski, P./Hahne, M.: Speichertechnologien für datenintensive Business-Intelligence-Anwendungen, in: Heilmann, H. et al. (Hrsg.): HMD – Praxis der Wirtschaftsinformatik: Business & Competitive Intelligence, o. Jg. (Februar 2006), Heft 247, S. 33-42

Jennings, M.: Information Delivery Shortcuts, Part 1, in: DM Review Magazine, Vol. 15 (April 2005), No. 4, pp. 46 – 47

Jennings, M.: Information Delivery Shortcuts, Part 2, in: DM Review Magazine, Vol. 15 (May 2005), No. 5, pp. 54 – 58

Jennings, M.: Information Delivery Shortcuts, Part 3, in: DM Review Magazine, Vol. 15 (June 2005), No. 6, pp. 64 – 66

Kemper, H.-G./Baars, H.: Business Intelligence und Competitive Intelligence – IT-basierte Managementunterstützung und markt-/wettbewerbsorientierte Anwendungen, in: Heilmann, H. et al. (Hrsg.): HMD – Praxis der Wirtschaftsinformatik: Business & Competitive Intelligence, o. Jg. (Februar 2006), Heft 247, S. 7-20

Küsters, U. et al.: Forecasting Software: Past, Present and Future, in: International Journal of Forecasting, Vol. 22 (2006), No. 3, pp. 599-615

Price, D. A.: The Dawn of a new Era: What's next in Business Intelligence?, in DM Review Magazine, Vol. 16 (Feb. 2006), No. 2, pp. 18-23

Seufert, S./Lehmann, P.: Business Intelligence – Status Quo und zukünftige Entwicklungen, in: Heilmann, H. et al. (Hrsg.): HMD – Praxis der Wirtschaftsinformatik: Business & Competitive Intelligence, o. Jg. (Februar 2006), Heft 247, S. 21–32

Winter, R./Gericke, A.: Teradata University Network – Ein Portal zur Unterstützung der Lehre in den Bereichen Business Intelligence, Data Warehousing und Datenbanken, in: Wirtschaftsinformatik, 48. Jg. (2006), Heft 4, S. 276 – 281

Zaima, A./Kashner, J.: A Data Mining Primer for the Data Warehouse Professional, in: Business Intelligence Journal, Vol. 8 (2003), No. 2, pp. 45–54

Internet Sources

Ariyachandra, T./Watson, H.: Benchmarks for BI and Data Warehousing Success, in: DM Review Magazine, Vol. 16 (Jan. 2006),
http://www.teradata.com/t/pdf.aspx?a=134008&b=145457 [14.02.2007]

Daddah, C.: A Metric's Journey, in: Teradata Magazine Special Report, November 2005,
http://www.teradata.com/images/tdmag/articles/2005/4Q/0504_tdmag_metric2.pdf, [22.01.2007]

Wu, J.: Empowering the information enterprise: Indicators of Successful Business Intelligence Solutions, in: DM Review Magazine, Vol. 16 (Dec. 2006), No. 12, http://www.dmreview.com/article_sub.cfm?articleId=1069936, [8.02.2007]

www.teradatauniversitynetwork.com/www.teradatastudentsnetwork.com

www.olapreport.com

Index

A

accuracy	69
architectural framework	3, 9, 35
area	26, 30, 41, 48, 51, 52

association rules *see* descriptive techniques

B

Balanced Scorecard	VII, 10, 11
benefits	43, 54, 59

BI VII, IX, X, 1, 3, 5, 6, 7, 8, 9, 10, 11, 12, 13, 14, 15, 28, 32, 41, 42, 43, 53, 54, 55, 56, 57, 58, 59, 60, 61, 63, 65, 66, 67, 68, 69, 70, 71, 72

definitions (literature)	5
working definition	7
Business intelligence	*see* BI

C

classification	*see* predictive techniques
clustering	*see* descriptive techniques
cube	20, 21, 25, 38, 39

D

dashboard	58

data
data model	X, 22, 24
metadata	5, 32, 33, 34, 38, 54, 60
raw data	3
semi-structured data	5
structured data	4, 5, 12, 52, 54
unstructured data	4, 5, 12, 51, 54

data mart X, 13, 26, 27, 28, 29, 35, 41, 42, 52, 61, 70, 71, 72

data mining X, 4, 9, 28, 35, 45, 46, 47, 48, 49, 51, 52, 61
descriptive techniques	48
predictive techniques	46
text mining	51
verification techniques	46
web mining	51

data warehouse VII, IX, 5, 8, 9, 13, 14, 15, 17, 18, 19, 20, 21, 22, 24, 25, 26, 27, 28, 30, 31, 32, 33, 34, 35, 38, 39, 41, 42, 43, 45, 50, 54
central DW	26
core DW	26, 28
virtual DW	26
DM	*see* data mart

E

EIS	VII, 9, 10, 54, 58
ETL	VII, IX, X, 8, 10, 18, 28, 30, 32, 33
aggregation	22, 30, 31, 33, 67
enrichment	30, 32, 33, 54
filtering	30, 31, 33, 38

harmonisation	30, 31, 33

F

financial forecasting	1
Ford Motor Company	66

I

information technology	VII, IX, 1, 6, 7, 33, 36, 67, 72

K

KM	VII, X, 13, 42, 53, 54, 56, 66, 67
knowledge IX, X, 1, 3, 5, 6, 8, 11, 13, 17, 35, 45, 51, 52, 53, 55, 56, 58, 59, 60, 63
Knowledge Management	*see* KM

M

MDBMS	VII, IX, 22, 25, 26, 29, 38
metadata	*see* data
MIS	VII, 9, 10, 11, 54, 58
multidimensional model	21, 22

O

ODS	VII, X, 13, 28, 35
OLAP	VII, IX, 9, 11, 26, 28, 35, 36, 37, 38, 39, 40, 41, 59, 65, 66, 69
definition	35
FASMI	36, 37
OLTP VIII, 11, 13, 15, 18, 19, 26, 30, 33, 35

P

pivot	39
portal	13, 53, 54, 55, 56, 57, 58

Q

queries	*see* query
query	VIII, IX, X, 6, 21, 22, 24, 26, 27, 31, 32, 35, 37, 41, 52, 59, 61

R

RDBMS	VIII, 21, 22, 25, 26, 28, 29, 38
redundancy	21, 24, 33
regression	*see* predictive techniques
relational model	20, 21
reporting IX, 6, 9, 11, 14, 28, 35, 36, 41, 42, 59
reports	1, 32, 38, 41, 42, 43, 56, 58, 59

S

sequence discovery	*see* descriptive techniques
snowflake scheme	22, 25, 37
star scheme	22, 23, 24, 25, 37

T

time series	*see* predictive techniques